Sweden and the Revival of the Welfare State

NEW THINKING IN POLITICAL ECONOMY
Series Editor: Peter J. Boettke, *George Mason University, USA*

New Thinking in Political Economy aims to encourage scholarship in the intersection of the disciplines of politics, philosophy and economics. It has the ambitious purpose of reinvigorating political economy as a progressive force for understanding social and economic change.

The series is an important forum for the publication of new work analysing the social world from a multidisciplinary perspective. With increased specialization (and professionalization) within universities, interdisciplinary work has become increasingly uncommon. Indeed, during the 20th century, the process of disciplinary specialization reduced the intersection between economics, philosophy and politics and impoverished our understanding of society. Modern economics in particular has become increasingly mathematical and largely ignores the role of institutions and the contribution of moral philosophy and politics.

New Thinking in Political Economy will stimulate new work that combines technical knowledge provided by the 'dismal science' and the wisdom gleaned from the serious study of the 'worldly philosophy'. The series will reinvigorate our understanding of the social world by encouraging a multidisciplinary approach to the challenges confronting society in the new century.

Titles in the series include:

Sweden and the Revival of the Capitalist Welfare State

Andreas Bergh

Lund University and the Research Institute of Industrial Economics, Sweden

NEW THINKING IN POLITICAL ECONOMY

Edward Elgar
PUBLISHING

Cheltenham, UK • Northampton, MA, USA

Published by
Edward Elgar Publishing Limited
The Lypiatts
15 Lansdown Road
Cheltenham
Glos GL50 2JA
UK

Edward Elgar Publishing, Inc.
William Pratt House
9 Dewey Court
Northampton
Massachusetts 01060
USA

Paperback edition 2016

A catalogue record for this book
is available from the British Library

Library of Congress Control Number: 2014938806

This book is available electronically in the **Elgar**online
Economics subject collection
DOI 10.4337/9781783473502

ISBN 978 1 78347 349 6 (cased)
ISBN 978 1 78347 350 2 (eBook)
ISBN 978 1 78643 510 1 (paperback)

Typeset by Servis Filmsetting Ltd, Stockport, Cheshire
Printed and bound in Great Britain by TJ International Ltd, Padstow

To my daughter Amanda

Contents

Figures, tables and boxes

FIGURES

TABLES

BOXES

Preface

In the spring of 2004 I was a visiting researcher in the United States. As a Swedish economist, I noticed a great deal of interest in Sweden among foreign academics. The knowledge of our small country is often impressive. The Swedish phenomenon is the source of admiration as well as surprise, and occasionally also criticism and scepticism. I quickly realized the value in being able to look at one's own country from a distance – and how difficult it is to convey an accurate and encompassing image of Sweden to social scientists from other countries.

This book is an attempt to shed light on Sweden as a 'capitalist welfare state', despite the seemingly contradictory nature of that description. Many Swedish achievements are the result of a clear line of demarcation between market and politics, while Sweden's problems often stem from blurring the line between the market sphere and the political sphere.

This is the third updated version of the book, and also the first version to be available in English. The number of people who have helped me at various stages in the process has become too large to list, but I do want to thank Assar, Daniel, Henrik (several Henriks actually), Magnus, Mi, Niclas, Nils, Pernilla, Pontus, Stig-Björn and Therese for friendly help and suggestions. At various times, Torsten and Ragnar Söderbergs Foundations have provided financial support.

Malmö, November 2013
Andreas Bergh

1. Introduction

Despite its modest population size, Sweden is an interesting country for social scientists worldwide. Some look at Sweden and see a frightening example of high taxes and a much too generous welfare state. Others point to largely the same things and see a role model. Sweden is or has been known for many different things. Some are myths: for example, Sweden never had the highest suicide rate in the world, but is in fact very close to the OECD average. Others used to be true but are no longer so: Swedish taxes were the highest in the Western world until around 2001, when Denmark overtook us. Recently, one of the most prominent features of Sweden has actually been rapid change: taxes have fallen, globalization has increased, unionization has fallen and inequality has increased.

At the beginning of the 1980s, the Swedish economy was a highly regulated and closed economy. Today, Sweden is one of the most globalized countries in the world. Over the past few decades, Sweden has been subject to one of the most rapid increases of globalization and economic liberalization in the world. When a great deal of change takes place over a relatively short period of time, it is easy to lose perspective. Outside Swedish borders, the perception of Sweden is often rather dated and, to some extent, still characterized by the Sweden of yesteryear. Then again, Swedes also become blind to their environment. For a long time, the debate in Sweden was dominated by economic problems and the fact that Sweden had lost its position as one of the richest countries in the world, ranked according to purchasing power per capita. Undoubtedly, this was an important debate, but when discussing the reasons for lagging behind during a period of roughly twenty-five years, we stand the risk of forgetting to draw lessons from the preceding one hundred years, which were very successful.

Between approximately 1870 and 1970 Sweden went from being one of Europe's poorest countries to being the fourth richest country in the world, after the US, Luxembourg and Switzerland. During roughly the same period Sweden also became one of the countries in the world where incomes are most evenly distributed across the population. This book begins with an attempt to explain this remarkable development.

The problematic period between 1970 and 1995 has been well covered in the literature. Sweden ran into trouble and the currency was devaluated repeatedly. Inequality started to spread and unemployment among young people began to rise. Nevertheless, this all happened at a slow pace, and started from low levels. A proper debate concerning Sweden's problems did not come about until the crisis of the 1990s was a fact. However, at this stage quite a few changes had already been completed. Between 1985 and 1997 in particular, the degree of capitalism, market economy and economic freedom increased in a variety of areas in Sweden. There was talk of system change and neoliberalism, but the welfare state and the high taxes persisted, albeit in a slightly different form: taxes remained high, but they became less progressive. Today, the welfare state is still universal, but allows more competition and freedom of choice.

Today, the picture of Sweden is mixed. Large parts of the economy have developed well for a long time, and public finances are among the best among Western democracies. Unemployment, however, remains a problem – especially among young people and immigrants. The final part of this book discusses the challenges ahead, and Sweden's potential to handle these problems through further reforms. Can the capitalist welfare state survive?

2. Prosperity and equality: the golden years 1870–1970

The period between 1870 and 1970 in Sweden was very successful.[1] Sweden achieved not only a very high level of material well-being (as measured by real GDP per capita), but also managed to have prosperity more evenly distributed across the population than most other countries. Some would surely say that income compression in Sweden went too far. In any case, the strong economic growth that Sweden experienced between 1870 and 1970 led to Sweden becoming not only one of the richest countries in the world, but also one of the most egalitarian.

In this chapter, the causes of Sweden's prosperity and the egalitarian income distribution are discussed. After describing and summarizing research that helps us understand the evolution of prosperity and relatively high income equality in Sweden, I ask to what extent the answers are to be found in what is known as the Swedish model. The conclusion will be that while the standard description of the Swedish model captures many important aspects, it does not fully explain how Sweden became both prosperous and relatively egalitarian. While the Swedish model emphasizes Swedish exceptionalism in dimensions such as labour movement organization and welfare state universality, the arguments presented in this chapter suggest that the origins of Sweden's economic success are less exceptional: just like most countries, Sweden grew rich because of well-functioning capitalist institutions, and the compressed Swedish income distribution seems to be much older than many of Sweden's progressive welfare state policies that were implemented in the 1970s.

HOW DID SWEDEN BECOME WEALTHY?

Sweden went from having a per capita income equivalent to 40–50 per cent of the United Kingdom's level during the first half of the nineteenth century to having 60–70 per cent of the UK's per capita income at the beginning of the twentieth century. The development continued and in

---

[1] As also noted by Lindbeck (2001) and Blomström and Kokko (2003).

3

Table 2.1   How much higher was GDP per hour worked in 1970 compared to 1870?

Country	Factor	Country	Factor
Sweden	17	USA	10
Japan	16	Denmark	9
Finland	14	Holland	7
Norway	12	United Kingdom	5
Germany	11	Australia	4

Source: Maddison (1982).

1970 Sweden was the fourth richest country in the world after Switzerland, the US and Luxembourg.[2] The period between 1870 and 1970 has been referred to as the golden years, and Table 2.1 explains why. Swedish productivity grew to 17 times its size during this period – a figure only to be remotely matched by Japan and Finland.[3]

The story of Sweden's economic history has been told many times.[4] But the accounts differ depending on the emphasis. A typical explanation of prosperity is based on the export of natural resources. When industrialism gained momentum in the UK, demand increased for Swedish timber and ore. Another explanation often mentioned is that Sweden benefited from staying out of the world wars.

One of the first to scrutinize these standard explanations was Swedish economist Johan Myhrman (1994). Surprisingly few have followed. If British economic development led to growth in Sweden, Myhrman asked, why was the Swedish economy so weak in its development between 1780 and 1860? And why was there an increase in Swedish economic growth around the turn of the last century, when the British economy had slowed down?

The standard explanations of Sweden's success cannot constitute the whole truth. Not only do they fail to answer the questions regarding timing that Myhrman raised; more fundamentally, they tell us very little regarding the fundamental causes of prosperity. Having valuable natural

---

[2] In the earlier versions of the OECD statistics over purchasing power, Sweden actually came in third. However, Luxembourg has now revised its GDP figures.

[3] Henrekson (1992) underlines that Sweden actually had high growth even during the 1950s and 1960s. The fact that the increases in productivity were marginally higher than in other countries during this period can be wholly explained by these countries' recovery after the Second World War. See also the debate between Krantz (2000) and Henrekson (2000).

[4] See for example Schön (2000) and Magnusson (2002).

resources is for sure no guarantee that a country will develop and prosper: many countries grow rich without being resource abundant, and many resource-abundant countries actually are better characterized by violent conflicts than by high economic growth.

Institutions and Prosperity

Today, most economists would agree that institutional factors must be taken into account, and many would argue that certain institutional arrangements are fundamental causes of long-run growth. An institutional perspective makes it easier to understand why Sweden had a successful period starting around 1870, and it is also useful for explaining why Sweden started trailing behind at the beginning of the 1970s.

It is only quite recently that an understanding of the role institutions play in the development of a society's economy has arisen in the field of economics. The so-called neoclassical growth models, stemming from Solow (1956), predict that growth per person increases when savings and investments increase. When savings are constant, the economy will grow at the same pace as technological development. An increase in investments can boost economic growth, but only temporarily while capital is accumulating. These models say nothing about what determines or influences the rate of technological development and thereby the long-term growth rate. Prosperity in these models is exogenous and left unexplained.

More recent theories take education, training and knowledge (human capital) into account as well – see for example Lucas (1988) and Romer (1990). If education is beneficial for society in general, and not only the individual who goes through schooling, these theories argue that there may be reason to finance education through taxation, and that doing so may actually increase the growth rate. However, the theories still lack an in-depth analysis of what it is that promotes innovation and the creation of new knowledge: the studies carried out often define education as the amount of years spent in school.

As early as 1973, North and Thomas (1973) had pointed to some problems with the way traditional economics explain growth, by noting that 'innovation, economies of scale, education, capital accumulation, etc. [. . .] are not causes of growth; they *are* growth' (p. 2, italics in original). In 1990, Douglas North defined institutions as the rules of the game that shape human interaction and argued that 'third world countries are poor because the institutional constraints define a set of payoffs to political/ economic activity that does not encourage productive activity.'[5] The focus

---

[5] North (1990, p. 110).

on institutions as rules of the game spurred research that tried to explicitly account for the role of institutions in research on economic growth. An important example is Knack and Keefer (1995) who added different indicators of the security of property rights to standard growth regressions and concluded that institutions that protect property rights are crucial to economic growth. They found that the security of property rights not only affects the magnitude of investment, but also the efficiency of the resource allocation.

Abdiweli (2003) has reviewed the existing research and confirms with his own research that judicial efficiency, low levels of corruption, well-organized public bureaucracy and well-defined private ownership co-vary with high growth. The risk of breach of contract and risk of government expropriation is particularly damaging according to Abdiweli's analysis. For a summary of research on the importance of property rights for economic growth, see Asoni (2008).

Many studies focus on specific institutions such as corruption and property rights and examine how these particular institutions affect economic development. In practice, many institutions typically go together. One strand of the literature has taken the approach of bundling institutions and policies that are expected to make markets work well under the label 'economic freedom'. Economic freedom refers not only to private property rights but also to rule of law in general, freedom to trade, absence of government interventionism and a stable monetary system. After surveying 52 studies of the relationship between various measures of economic freedom and growth, Doucouliagos and Ulubasoglu (2006) concluded that economic freedom has a robust positive effect on economic growth.[6]

The mechanisms behind the relationship between stable capitalist institutions and growth are easy to understand: the individual who is in a position to work, trade or be innovative wants to know which rules apply concerning contracts, agreements, profits and wages. For the same reason, it is important to be sure about the value of money in the future. Uncertainty and the risk of violent conflicts can make investments and work effort too risky to undertake. The effect of institutions on economic development can thus be understood as a result of decreasing transaction costs and decreasing uncertainty (Berggren et al., 2012; Kingston and Caballero, 2009).

Research on the role of institutions can also explain what sometimes is referred to as the curse of the natural resources, namely why a surprising number of poor countries nevertheless have quite a few valuable natural resources. In the absence of good institutions, these valuable natural

---

[6] A similar type of bundling is done under the label Quality of Government.

BOX 2.1   THE LINK BETWEEN INSTITUTIONS AND GROWTH: CORRELATION OR CAUSATION?

Can it be verified that the relationship between institutions and growth is causal, in the sense that institutions cause growth rather than the other way round? The institutions (that is, the rules and norms) of any society are typically chosen and enforced by the people in that society. It is thus possible that as societies grow richer, they are more likely to implement a certain type of institutions – in which case the empirical evidence that certain institutions are good for growth might be based on reverse causality!

Researchers have met this challenge using a variety of approaches. One strand of the literature uses pure theory and formal analysis to show that profit-seeking individuals invest less if others can seize the fruits of their investments (Demsetz, 1967).

A second approach is to do detailed case studies trying to identify the mechanisms that hinder growth. In his famous book *The Mystery of Capital*, De Soto (2000) sheds light on how the absence of functioning property rights explains the lack of growth in the world's poorest countries: when houses cannot be mortgaged because they were built without permits, investments fail to materialize. Ambiguous property rights cause resources to be put into the handling of conflicts instead of into prosperity-enhancing production.

Another, third type of research relies on cross-country regressions. In some cases reverse causality can be deemed unlikely by looking closely at the timing of changes, verifying that the cross-country correlation is not explained by rich countries increasing economic freedom when they are already rich (Heckelman, 2000; Dawson, 2003). A more common strategy is to use so-called instrumental variables to create a quasi-natural experiment. Some well-known examples include Acemoglu et al. (2001) using variation in malaria mortality among European settlers, Mauro (1995) using ethno-linguistic fractionalization and Easterly and Levine (2003) using latitude. The idea underlying this approach is that the instrument is not caused by the outcome examined (in this case economic growth) but has an impact on the outcome by having an impact on certain institutions.

The fourth approach uses natural experiments, that is situations when lucky circumstances create a situation similar to an experiment in the sense that a control group can be used to evaluate the impact of a certain institutional arrangement. An example is the situation when some, but not all, squatters in Buenos Aires were given formal property rights to their land in 1984, which led to significant and sizeable effects on housing investment and child education in the 2000s, as reported by Galiani and Schargrodsky (2010). Similar evidence exists for the beneficial causal effect of successfully fighting corruption, identified using a newspaper anti-corruption campaign in Uganda by Svensson and Reinikka (2005).

Valid criticism can be raised against all four approaches. Pure theory might not teach us anything about the real world. Case studies can be dismissed as just story telling. Instrumental variables rarely produce completely random exogenous variation, and it is typically hard to ensure that the instrument affects the outcome only through its impact on institutional arrangements. Finally, even perfect natural experiments can be questioned on the basis of external validity: property rights may be beneficial for squatters in Buenos Aires, but how do we know that similar effects would appear in other contexts?

Still, with theoretical evidence, case studies, cross-country empirics and natural experiments all pointing in the same direction, the case for property rights and low corruption being good for economic development, is close to as solid as it gets in the social sciences.

resources cause conflicts, corruption and other detrimental behaviour which offsets growing prosperity. On the other hand, when there are both laws and social norms that ease conflict resolution and create incentives for productive investments, natural resources are more likely to be put to productive use – see for example Mehlum et al. (2006).

The Role of Institutions in Sweden

Sweden's economic expansion during the golden years of 1870 to 1970 is no puzzle, but rather a case study illustrating the importance of institutions. Certainly, Sweden benefited from industrialization in Britain, and, without doubt, Swedish timber and ore played an important role in

Swedish exports. But without certain institutional reforms, Sweden would not have been able to benefit from these factors in the same way.

The land reforms in the farming sector are a natural starting point for describing institutional reforms in Sweden. As described by Heckscher (1942) they began, and were most radical, in Scania, where land during the late eighteenth century was rearranged from being a patchwork of plots to organized squares of land set around centrally placed farms. At the beginning of the nineteenth century similar changes took place throughout the country.

When first carried out, the land reforms were not popular. But it was soon recognized that they led to increased possibilities and incentives for land improvements. Apart from the practical benefits from abandoning the patchwork of plots, land reforms were successful because they changed the incentives for peasants. The secure property rights among landowners combined with fixed taxes provided strong incentives to improve agricultural productivity, for example by using crop variation, trenching and the removal of stones. The situation was different for those peasants who were tenants under the nobility, where rising rents and the threat of eviction hindered investments. In some cases, the land reforms increased resource equality by allocating land more equally. The idea was that every farmer would be allocated approximately the same amount of connected land. The land reforms increased resource equality and created opportunities and incentives for more individuals to partake in production and economic life. Such resource equality can be an important growth factor, which is emphasized by Gunnarsson and Rojas (2004) in their analysis of the problems that developing countries face today.

The effect of property rights and the changes in the incentive structure that land reforms induced has been documented by Olsson and Svensson (2010) using data covering on average 450 farms each year from 1702 to 1864. Their conclusion is that property rights play a crucial part in explaining the rising agricultural production. The land reforms were working and the acreage of cultivated land in Sweden was doubled during the first half of the nineteenth century.

In the mid-nineteenth century, the financial system also developed strongly. Private commercial and savings banks were established in Sweden, and they were able to lend money to the private sector. After some important deregulations of the credit market, these became important sources of credit for the private sector, which facilitated savings for farmers and benefited private investment. The role of the Swedish Central Bank in granting credit to the private sector rapidly decreased (Larsson and Lindgren, 1989). In 1840, the Swedish Central Bank's (Riksbanken) granting of credit to the private sector was three times as large as that of the other commercial banks – but this changed rapidly and the number of loans from commercial banks increased.[7]

Schön (2000) describes how for a long time regulations and export duties prevented timber from becoming an export product in itself: instead it had primarily been regarded as something necessary in order to produce iron. This changed during the 1840s when there was a reduction of both regulations and duties. Along the same lines, Jörnmark (2004) attributes much importance to liberalization in explaining the breakthrough of the forestry economy. He points out that it was not the older Swedish individuals in the more inland parts of the country who closed down their smelting-houses to open sawmills instead. Rather, it was often immigrant British, Norwegians and Germans along the Swedish coast who were responsible for the changes that transpired. Private property rights made it possible to buy land from old works and from the state through a selling-off process (*avvittrings-processen*). From the state's viewpoint, the selling of forest land was a way to create taxable units. The creation of private property rights thus contributed to timber generating profits for both the state and the capitalists.[8]

Freedom of trade also increased when the guild system was abolished in a first step in 1846. Prior to the system's abolition, it was required that all craftsmen start as apprentices (a possibility reserved for boys born within wedlock only) and finish their training by passing the examination for the master craftsman's diploma.

Schön sums up the effect of liberalization between 1850 and 1870 as Sweden gaining freedom of movement for people, goods and capital, both within and across its borders. Why it happened during this particular period is open to discussion. On the one hand, the prime minister and the minister of finance at the time, Louis De Geer and Johan August Gripenstedt, were free traders in the spirit of Adam Smith and French economist Frederic Bastiat, and Norberg (1999) argues that there was substantial ideological influence of liberal ideas in Sweden at the time. On the other hand, Lewin (1992) points out that Sweden was under pressure from the US and a number of European states to liberalize trade. According to Lewin, the tariff reductions in the 1850s were intended as a short-term measure during the intensive economic boom of that decade, but free trade

---

[7] Again, the question of causality is central: does a well-developed financial system promote growth, or does growth induce countries to improve their financial systems? Theoretically, the link can go both ways. For the case of Sweden, Hansson and Jonung (2000) suggest that during the period of 1890 to 1939, the financial system had an influence on both quantity and quality of investments, and was a contributing factor to the strong economic growth.

[8] In addition to Jörnmark (2004), see also the history of the timber industry, available at www.skogssverige.se (also in English).

remained in place until 1888, when European farming faced competition from American pork, paving the way for increased protectionism in Sweden and in Europe.

In order to have export-headed economic growth, one naturally needs to have goods to export. The focus on timber and ore easily lets one forget that Sweden, during the late nineteenth century, was an innovative nation, which in turn was aided by the existence of patent laws. The first Swedish patent law came in 1834, with important improvements added in 1856 and 1884. A number of patents soon became well-known Swedish export successes: Carl Richard Nyberg's patented blowtorch from 1881; Frans Wilhelm Lindqvist's patented paraffin stove run on compressed air from 1882 (the so-called Primus stove); Johan Petter Johansson's adjustable spanner patent in 1892; and Lars Magnus Ericsson's hand-micro telephone, invented in 1884 and patented in 1895. In 1891 Jonas Wenström patented three phase alternating current (important for Asea, and later ABB).[9]

Shortly after these economic liberalizations, Sweden experienced what Rothstein (2011) calls an indirect big bang against corruption. Though the meaning of an indirect big bang remains unclear, Rothstein notes that several important anti-corruption measures were implemented during a fairly short period of time: in 1845, Sweden introduced freedom of the press and the last formal aristocratic prerogative for higher positions in the State was abolished. Around the same time, several new public boards and agencies were established for carrying out investments in infrastructure, creating a need for technical skills among civil servants, which in turn paved the way for meritocratic recruitment of civil servants. Between 1855 and 1860, there were major revisions of the wage system in the civil service. Before the introduction of the new system, civil servants were often hired without sufficient funds to pay them, leading to some tolerance for civil servants accepting side payments from peasants. When the wage system was in place, and when meritocratic recruitment introduced, it became less acceptable to use public positions for the purpose of extracting rents. In 1862 a new criminal code includes a law on misconduct in office. In 1868, direct payments for services to individual civil servants were abolished, and in 1869, parliament decided that taxes must be paid in money instead of in goods. In all, it seems as if sometime between 1850 and 1900 Sweden succeeded with something very rare: decreasing the level of corruption.[10]

---

[9] Westholm (2009).

[10] The reforms mentioned by Rothstein (2011) are largely the same as those mentioned by Myhrman (1994), and also the same as those mentioned in textbooks such as Schön (2000).

Finally, a factor worth mentioning is the migration from Sweden to the United States. Between 1850 and 1930, 1.2 million Swedes emigrated, and the vast majority did not return. Nevertheless, the fact that some emigrants did actually return and the flow of ideas transmitted from emigrants via the so-called 'America letters', is an overlooked factor in Sweden's economic development, according to Henricson and Lindblad (1995) as well as Johnson (1997). Capital from personal savings and ideas from the United States were often turned into successful business ventures in Sweden.[11]

Institutional theories go far in explaining the events of the twentieth century. The positive growth in the 1950s and 1960s is usually attributed to successful macro-policies – but Myhrman points out that Sweden during this period also was greatly helped by the fixed exchange rate via the Bretton Woods system as well as an increase in trade through the General Agreement on Tariffs and Trade (GATT).

This analysis of Sweden resembles the analysis by North and Weingast (1989) of Britain. They put forward the argument that a number of institutional changes from 1680 rendered the state authority predictable in their actions: private property rights were maintained and confiscatory government interventions became fewer. This led to a predictability which was useful to tradesmen. Trade, in turn, entails mutually gainful exchanges, specialization profits, and more rapid spreading of new knowledge. Fresh knowledge and new innovations in turn create opportunities for further trade, and thus a positive growth spiral is generated. Hence, the institutional changes towards a market economy and a state governed by the rule of law were important factors in turning Britain into the centre of the industrial revolution.

The focus on the above institutions should not be taken to imply that other factors were not important. Research on economic growth also points to other intuitively plausible factors, such as infrastructure investments (for example, public spending on communications) and basic education; see for example Canning and Pedroni (2004) and Barro (1990). These areas were also reformed in Sweden during the nineteenth century. In the mid-nineteenth century, compulsory elementary school was introduced and railways were expanded. In addition, men and women were given equal rights of inheritance, which furthered women's active participation in the economy. Anton (1969) accounts for another very important factor, namely the spirit of consensus, predictability and rationality, which has largely characterized Swedish politics during the twentieth century.

---

[11] Johnson (1997) mentions, for instance, Walfrid Weibull from Scania who in 1870 started a seed-growing business after having come into contact with modern plant-breeding techniques in the US.

A full understanding of Sweden's impressive economic development since 1870 requires that standard explanations regarding timber, ore and the absence of war be complemented by institutional factors, in particular those relating to property rights, free trade and low corruption. The short summary in Box 2.2 recapitulates some of the important institutional changes which contributed to the Swedish success.

HOW DID SWEDEN BECOME EGALITARIAN?

When and why did Swedish poverty levels and income disparities decrease? The question is surprisingly unexplored, but by putting together a number of different contributions, a coherent picture emerges. To start with, we know that the development towards a more equal distribution of living standards started a long time ago.

When did Sweden Become Egalitarian?

Reliable data on inequality in any country before the 1960s are rare, but several different sources suggest that material inequality in Sweden started to fall a long time ago. Soltow (1989) calculates Gini coefficients for the value of rural land in Sweden in 1805, 1845, 1879 and in 1921, and notes a continuous decrease from 0.70 to 0.58. Roine and Waldenström (2008) study income tax return forms from the top 10 and top 1 per cent of the highest income earners, and conclude as follows:

> [ ] starting from levels of inequality approximately equal to those in other Western countries at the time, the income share of the Swedish top decile drops sharply over the first eighty years of the twentieth century. Most of the decrease takes place before the expansion of the welfare state and by 1950 Swedish top income shares were already lower than in other countries. (p. 366)

A similar outcome, although relating to the lower end of the income scale, is found by Rauhut (2002), who has studied the allocation of social security payments during the period of 1918 to 1997. After an increase in social security payments during the crisis in the 1930s, the number of people living off welfare continuously fell until 1965 – despite the fact that the real level of the benefit norm increased significantly during the same period. Finally, Bentzel (1952) documented a substantial compression of the distribution of disposable income between 1935 and 1948.

Hence, during the first part of the twentieth century Sweden experienced both a reduction of top incomes as well as a reduction of poverty. Swedish

BOX 2.2   EXAMPLES OF IMPORTANT
           INSTITUTIONAL REFORMS IN SWEDEN
           UNTIL THE 1900s

In the late 1700s, land reforms improved agricultural productivity.
1809: imperial rule ended and Sweden returned to a balanced
and stable division of power between the king and the Swedish
parliament (*Riksdag*). A number of Swedish Central Bank reforms
were implemented during the nineteenth century, including the
Central Bank's monopoly on the issuing of banknotes from **1903**
onwards, which in many respects led the Swedish Central Bank
to resemble a modern central bank at the beginning of the twentieth century.
1826: an institute of technology was established in Stockholm
(which in **1876** was converted into The Royal Institute of
Technology).
1842: compulsory elementary school was introduced.
1845: equal rights of inheritance for men and women were introduced.
1862: municipalities replaced parishes, and regulated municipal
autonomy was introduced.
1846: compulsory guild training was abolished, and general
freedom of trade ensued in **1864**.
During primarily the 1850s and 1860s, free trade reforms were
carried out in the form of lowered tariffs.
In the 1850s, standard rate postage within Sweden was introduced and played an important role in developing newspaper
distribution and consequently literacy.
Between 1856 and 1866, the infrastructure was improved through
the expansion of state-owned railways, which also prompted a
shift to standardized time in Sweden in **1879**.
During the 1860s, interest rate control was removed and banks
set up as limited companies were allowed.
1866: the four-estate system is abolished, establishing a modern
bicameral parliament.
1868: direct payments for services to individual civil servants is
abolished. From now on, the fee/money should no longer belong
to the individual civil servant but be state property.
1873: the Swedish Krona was introduced, replacing the
Riksdaler.

The Krona's value was tied to the gold standard, which provided a stability that made overseas trading easier.
1895: the Companies Act modernized legislation and responsibility was transferred to the newly established Patent and Registration Office.

Source: Myhrman (1994), Schön (2000) and Rothstein (2011).

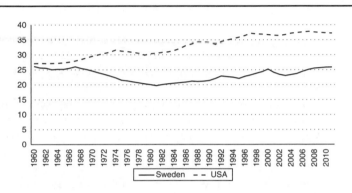

Source: SWIID 4.0, Solt (2008).

Figure 2.1   Gini for disposable household income in Sweden and the US 1960–2011

income distribution became compressed, which resulted in a middle class of considerable size compared to other countries.[12]

For more recent years, data on the income distribution are available in several publicly available databases such as the Standardized World Income Inequality Database (SWIID) compiled by Solt (2008).

As can be seen in Figure 2.1, the trend towards decreasing income inequality ended in Sweden around 1980. Since then, inequality in Sweden has increased at roughly the same rate as in the US (as noted by Gottschalk, 1997 and many others).[13] From an international perspective,

---

[12] Defining middle class as households having an income between 75 per cent and 125 per cent of median household income, Pressman (2007) calculates that 47 per cent of Swedish households belong to the middle class, compared to 29 per cent in the United States, 32 per cent in the UK (and an average 37 per cent among 11 Western democracies).

[13] Rauhut (2002) also notes a 193 per cent increase in the share of the population living off welfare between 1965 and 1997, despite the social benefit norm during this period remaining constant or slightly decreasing.

Sweden still has very low levels of inequality: in 2004–05, Sweden had the second lowest inequality of disposable income in the OECD (after Denmark), but in 2009–10, Denmark, Slovenia, Czech Republic, Norway, Belgium, Iceland, Finland, Slovak Republic and Austria all had lower inequality of disposable income among adults (18–65 years).

Why did Sweden Become Egalitarian?

Because the development towards an egalitarian distribution started over 200 years ago, and because Sweden in the 1950s was already more equal than comparable countries, the political arrangements that were put in place during the 1970s and later can hardly hold the key to explaining Swedish income equality. The major explanations must be sought further back in history.

As with economic growth, there is a standard explanation offered for the rise of equality in Sweden: a well-organized labour movement which provided Sweden with an effective labour market and a redistributing welfare state. And just as with the case of economic growth, the standard explanation does not tell the whole story.

Research on the determinants of poverty and inequality has identified a number of factors which promote equality. Several of these factors are relevant for Sweden. Many point towards the land reforms, trade unions, school reforms and the supply of well-educated labour, the early introduction of social insurance and women entering the labour force all having played a central role in shaping the Swedish income distribution.

Land reforms, hard work and private savings
The land reforms discussed above (page 9) were not only beneficial for economic development in general. Many authors have noted that land reforms also made it possible for poor farmers to escape poverty by virtue of increasing agricultural productivity (Jörberg, 1976; Soltow, 1989; Olsson and Svensson, 2010). A government report (Finanskommitten, 1863) also stressed that an increase in the number of savings banks was important for equality by aiding the private savings in poor households. This explanation is supported by Soltow (1989) who notes that the group with positive savings in the rural sector increased steadily after 1840. To put it simply: hard work and private savings made it possible for many poor farmers to escape poverty.

Trade unions
It is intuitive that when trade unions negotiate collectively for large groups of employees, the result will be smaller wage differences than otherwise.

The mechanism is confirmed by Bradley et al. (2003) who find that countries with more powerful trade union movements (measured as union memberships) have greater equality in gross earnings. Using the same data, Moller et al. (2003) also find correlation between strong trade unions and low levels of relative poverty.

The emergence of Swedish trade unions at the end of the nineteenth century and the mutual recognition between the Swedish Employers Confederation (SAF) and the Swedish Trade Union Confederation (LO) in 1906 is thus a plausible contributing factor to the increase in equality. The decrease in inequality during the twentieth century also coincided with growing trade union membership. According to Lundh (2002) the number of blue-collar workers belonging to a trade union rose heavily during the first 50 years of the twentieth century to reach approximately 80 per cent. With a slight delay, the number of white-collar workers belonging to a trade union followed the same trend, but reached 80 per cent first in the 1970s. Unionization peaked at 85 per cent in 1993, and since then trade union memberships have dropped slightly, with sharp decreases in 2007 and 2008. Since 2009, unionization has been roughly constant at 70 per cent.[14]

School reforms

Compulsory primary schooling plays a fundamental role in how the welfare state promotes income equality. First, the distribution of expenditure on primary schooling is generally evenly distributed among all (as opposed to expenditure on higher education – see Bergh, 2007). Even when financed using completely proportional taxes, school spending will be redistributive. Secondly, basic education is a typical example of a benefit with a 'counterfactual equality effect': if compulsory primary schooling had not existed, children from well-off families would have acquired similar knowledge from their parents. This would, to a much lesser extent, have been the case for children in families with lower socio-economic status.

Very convincing empirical support for these theoretical mechanisms is provided by Meghir and Palme (2005) who study the Swedish compulsory school reform of the 1950s, which introduced a uniform, compulsory nine-year school with national standardized tests. The reform lends itself well to being evaluated, as a number of municipalities ran both the old and the new school system simultaneously for several student cohorts. The results are clear: the introduction of a uniform, compulsory school made students more inclined to go on to upper secondary school. The increase was greater among students with fathers who had a low level of education.

[14] Kjellberg (2011).

Meghir and Palme also studied the effect on future incomes, and show that the school reform clearly benefited those children with fathers who had a low level of education. For those children with well-educated fathers, the reform actually had a negative impact on their future earnings. Having access to IQ data, Meghir and Palme show that the reform was particularly constructive for gifted children whose fathers had a low level of education.

Hence, there is strong evidence to suggest that the school reform led to an increase in income equality in Sweden: owing to the reform, the distribution of human capital is more equal than it would have been if students, to a greater extent, had been dependent on the family and market for basic schooling. Similar conclusions are reached by Brunello et al. (2009) studying variation across 12 European countries and over time in the changes of the minimum school leaving age.[15]

There are no data available to carry out a similar assessment of the 1842 elementary school statute, which required every parish to have an elementary school. It is, however, likely that the effects were akin to those of the reform studied by Meghir and Palme. Many children were put through school prior to the introduction of the elementary school statute. Thus, the reform was of particular importance to those children who otherwise, and usually with great difficulty, would have had to obtain similar knowledge elsewhere.

Education emerges as an explanatory factor also when Lindbeck (1998) discusses Swedish equality. According to Lindbeck, research shows that the narrowing of the wage gap came about as a result of an increase in the supply of well-educated labour, in combination with the solidaric wage policy of the Rehn–Meidner model (see page 25).

Social insurance

As pointed out by Edebalk (2000) there is a misunderstanding that the distinct Swedish social insurance model was introduced in the 1930s and 1940s. In fact, the foundations were laid a lot earlier. Edebalk mentions the government grants given to the health insurance funds in 1891, compulsory employer responsibility for work-related injuries, and the national pensions system (of the basic security type) which was introduced in 1913.[16] Moreover, 1916 saw the introduction of industrial injury insurance, which established the principle of income security being in Sweden

---

[15] See also Bjorklund et al. (2009) who show that the importance of family background for personal income decreased for men born between 1932 and 1968, and suggest that primary school reforms are likely explanations.

[16] An important explanation of why the issue of pensions became important at this time was that the share of the population older than 65 had increased from 4.8 per cent in 1850 to

(also known as Bismarckian social insurance systems), where the benefit is defined as a replacement rate based on the income lost. National sickness benefit was not introduced until 1955, in a very limited manner (Edebalk, 2006).

The redistributive effects that stem from social insurance are complicated. Simply put, social insurance can increase equality by forcing high-risk groups and low-risk groups to be part of the same insurance scheme, where the insurance premium is based on the average risk. For instance, the sickness benefit insurance redistributes money from those who are rarely sick to those who are sick often. In practice, high-income earners are typically sick less often than others, and therefore the risk pooling effect also leads to redistribution from high-income earners to low-income earners. With occupational injury insurance, money is redistributed in a similar way, from those who do not get injured to those who do suffer work-related injuries. A nationwide, compulsory insurance is therefore particularly beneficial to those individuals who work in more injury-prone work places.

Here, two points immediately need to be stressed. First, the advantage of having insurance is the security that comes from knowing that you are insured. This benefit is enjoyed by all who are insured, regardless of how often accidents actually occur. Second, it is not obvious that the groups who are net payers to social insurance would be able to find better insurance on private insurance markets. A private insurance company can offer cheap insurance contracts to individuals who are at low risk of falling ill, only if they can avoid high-risk individuals from purchasing these contracts – otherwise the insurance will run at a loss. When risks are difficult to observe, this can turn out to be very expensive, complicated or even impossible, and as a result the low-risk group may actually be better off under mandatory social insurance.[17]

The most extensive Swedish social insurance structure is the pensions system. In what sense is the pension system an insurance? The answer is that the risk managed by a pensions system is the risk of living until an unexpectedly old age without having sufficient savings. In general, living longer than expected has to be regarded as a pleasant surprise. But turning 85 is less pleasant if your savings are gone by the time you reach 80. A pension insurance spreads these risks across all insured, and a public pension system can spread them across the entire population. The effect

8.4 per cent in 1900. This was, in turn, an immediate effect of the emigration from Sweden to the US during this period.

[17] On the private insurance market, the problem is caused by asymmetrical information: the insurance taker has more information about his/her level of risk than the insurance company. For further reading, see for example Kreps (1990) or Barr (1998).

is that money on average flows from the short-lived to the long-lived: from men to women, from blue-collar workers to white-collar workers, from smokers to non-smokers. But these redistributive effects are only applicable on average and *ex post*. During each individual's lifetime, he or she will benefit from knowing that their consumption is secured for as long as they live – though some will die long before retirement.[18] Hence, those who benefit from the pensions system are the individuals who would have had difficulties acquiring this type of security in any other way.

Female labour participation

Johansson (2006) notes that the decrease in income inequality during the 1950s and 1960s was driven by income compression among women as female labour participation increased. Most scholars now seem to agree that this development was not driven by an ideological desire for gender equality, but rather a consequence of economic growth and a shortage of labour – as described for example by Berntsson (2002). This led to an expansion of public child care facilities, a policy supported by both the employers' association and by the trade unions. Increasing gender equality and income equality in general were thus two side-effects of policies mainly motivated by the need to increase labour supply.

What about progressive taxes?

At first thought, it seems reasonable that progressive taxation plays an important part in promoting income equality. But several scholars have noted that the combination of proportional taxes and universal benefits can create substantial redistribution from high-income earners to low-income earners – provided that the size of the redistributive sector is large (see Åberg, 1989 and also Rothstein, 1998). What is important for redistribution, is that public spending covers what low-income earners would otherwise have had difficulties in obtaining.

For example, the equality-promoting effect of primary schooling or publicly provided child care that facilitate female labour force participation requires stable sources of tax revenue – but not necessarily progressive taxes. In fact, because having a large tax financed public sector requires high levels of tax revenue, universal welfare states typically tax most of the population relatively highly, compared to countries with smaller public sectors, where high-income earners are typically taxed much more in relative terms, as can be seen in Appendix E.

This logic applies very much to Sweden, where redistribution is not

---

[18] The age of retirement set in the system in 1913 was 67 years of age. At that point, the average life span was 56 years.

primarily due to progressive taxation. In fact the biggest sources of tax revenue in Sweden are taxes that are roughly proportional: payroll tax, national insurance contributions, and VAT (*mervärdesskatten*, the so-called *moms*). Before the earned income tax credit introduced in 2007, this also applied to local income tax. The state level income tax is clearly progressive, but it actually constitutes only a small part of the tax revenue, as seen below in Table 4.1.

Social mobility and capitalist dynasties?

Sweden and the Nordic countries in general are known for having high levels of social mobility in the sense that family background plays a relatively minor role in determining people's economic outcomes in general. This was recently confirmed by Björklund et al. (2012). They also note, however, that mobility is much lower within the top per-centile of the population, and that the most likely mechanism for this is inherited wealth. It thus seems as if relatively high levels of income equality in Sweden coexist with what Björklund et al. call capitalistic dynasties. This finding is in line with the fact that policies in Sweden for a long time favoured concentration of firms and concentration of private ownership (Henrekson and Jakobsson, 2001). One might specu-late that the success of Swedish capitalism lies partly in the combination of these capitalistic dynasties with high levels of income equality for a large middle class.[19] It is also interesting to note that the recent trend towards increasing inequality in Sweden seems to be largely driven by increases in capital gains at the very top of the distribution (Roine and Waldenström, 2008).

What Kind of Equality is Desirable?

There are many reasons why equality is desirable. In addition to purely normative arguments, there is a well-established negative correlation between inequality and lower social trust (Jordahl, 2008) and an ongoing discussion on the adverse health consequences of income inequality (Subramanian and Kawachi, 2004; Kondo et al., 2012). Still, it is worth thinking critically about the way equality and inequality are measured and used, both in political and academic debates.

Equality is typically measured by comparing the difference in people's annual incomes in any given year, and the underlying assumption is often that smaller differences are preferable. But it is not obvious that the most

---

[19] For some anecdotal evidence on the role of capitalistic dynasties in Sweden still today, see af Kleen (2009).

relevant time span to measure is one year, or that it is actually incomes that should be measured. Nor is it normatively obvious that differences should always be minimized.

A common objection against the standard approach of measuring yearly incomes is that equality should apply to the distribution of resources or opportunities, rather than to the distribution of incomes. A reoccurring notion in political philosophy is that differences which stem from circumstances beyond a person's control should ideally not exist, while differences that stem from free choice should remain. Of course, this position rests on the assumption that it is possible to separate circumstances beyond one's control from individual choices, the consequences of which the individual should be held responsible for. Examining how well different countries satisfy a certain version of equality of opportunity, Sweden differs so markedly from the other countries that the authors question whether it has moved beyond the notion of equal opportunities and instead is aiming for equality of outcome – see Roemer (2002).

Another objection is that inequality measured as disparity in the income distribution is less interesting than the actual welfare of those worst off in society or the share of the poor in the population. Poverty can be measured in absolute terms (which suggests that rich countries have very few, if any, poor) or in relative terms (which means that even rich countries can have significant poverty, if many household incomes fall below 50 per cent of the median income, which is a common definition of poverty).

The focus on incomes can of course be explained by the relative ease with which incomes can be measured, especially when compared to concepts such as 'opportunities' and 'quality of life' which are difficult to define. Questions regarding what differences in income are acceptable, and if it is income disparity, absolute or relative poverty which should be minimized, are ultimately normative questions. However, the time span measurement of a year is still arbitrary, as it would be just as possible to compare hourly wages, monthly income or income over longer time periods.

An argument for choosing to measure a shorter time span, such as hourly wages, is that income disparity over longer periods of time can partly be explained by people simply choosing to work different amounts during this period. In simple terms, hourly pay depends on how valuable the work that an individual can manage during an hour is to the person paying, while hours worked is, to a varying extent, an individual choice to be made within the restrictions set by legislation on working hours, holiday days, and what the employer is willing to accept.

One effect of comparing annual incomes is that some inequality will be registered simply for the reason that people are of different ages and therefore have reached different stages in their careers. An increase in population growth or salaries that rise faster during a career can lead to enhanced inequalities on a yearly basis – even if everybody's lifetime incomes were identical. Further, this type of measurement does not differentiate between low incomes that are due to involuntary poverty and those that are due to extended leave from work to study or travel.

If incomes are compared over a longer period of time, the level of inequality is significantly lower than when measured on an annual basis. According to Björklund (1993) the inequality of total lifetime incomes is approximately 40 per cent lower than for annual incomes. Absent data on lifetime income, a useful alternative might be to use inequality of consumption rather than yearly income, as consumption may tell us more about actual living standards than an annual income any given year could do.

Finally, it should be pointed out that income differences serve as important signals, indicating what type of labour is in high demand. Income disparities can also have desirable effects in the long run if they strengthen incentives for education and employment.

Despite all the objections outlined above, there are also some advantages to annual income disparity as a measure of inequality: apart from being relatively easy to define and measure, it seems that many politicians and voters see an intrinsic value in low annual income disparity. There is also a rather widespread theory regarding so-called *relative deprivation*, according to which people compare themselves to others in their surrounding environment, and dislike coming out unfavourably – see Runciman (1966) and Yitzhaki (1982).

Nevertheless, the discussion concerning different methods of measuring inequality is not decisive in the Swedish case: after the golden years of substantial growth 1870–1970, Sweden experienced low levels of inequality almost regardless of how it is measured. Moving on, let us take a look at when and why this happened.

IS SWEDEN EXCEPTIONAL?

To what extent can Sweden's prosperity and income distribution be explained by the so-called 'Swedish model'? To answer this question, the model must be defined. A review of the literature in which the concept is used reveals several different definitions of the model – but there are also a number of similarities.[20] The Swedish model often refers to one or more of the following four features:

[20] The following pages are, to a large extent, based on Magnusson (2002), Schön (2000) and Björklund (1982).

BOX 2.3   THE COUNTERFACTUAL
          PROBLEM: CAN WE MEASURE THE
          REDISTRIBUTIVE EFFECT OF THE
          WELFARE STATE?

To evaluate the redistributive effect of the welfare state properly, we need to know what the income distribution would be in the absence of the welfare state. In other words, a counterfactual situation is needed for comparison with the outcome when the welfare state is present. Because this counterfactual is not observed, many scholars use the actual distribution with taxes and transfers subtracted as a counterfactual. For example, Smeeding and Sandström (2005) calculate that before taxes and pensions, 82 per cent of pensioners in Sweden would be below the poverty threshold, but due to pension payments the actual number poverty rate is only 8 per cent. Surely this does not mean that pension payments reduce poverty by more than 70 per cent, but Smeeding and Sandström actually make this mistake – and so do several scholars who have tried to measure the redistributive effect of the welfare state by comparing the income distribution before and after taxes and transfers (sometimes called the pre-fisc/post-fisc approach). The problem is that if the pension system did not exist, people would behave differently, perhaps work longer and most likely ensure higher additional incomes from private savings. The measure of redistribution is inflated by the fact that Swedish pensions are high, and that pensioners have trusted them to actually be paid out. Similarly, the Gini coefficient for income with taxes and transfers subtracted is not a good measure of what the income distribution would be in the absence of taxes and transfers. For example, as already mentioned, publicly financed schooling increases income equality by affecting the distribution of human capital – but because schooling affects the income distribution both before and after taxes, the effect will not be captured by the difference between the two distributions. Also, taxes and transfers will impact how much people earn, and whether people work, retire or leave the labour force to care for family – see further Uusitalo (1985) and Bergh (2005) and the summary by Brady and Sosnaud (2009) who actually suggest that 'moving away from discourse of redistribution' would be a productive step for research in this area (p. 535).

The obvious alternative is to measure directly what matters: inequality or poverty based on the disposable income. After all, this is the reality actually lived in, and it can be measured and observed without making strong assumptions about unobservable counterfactuals.

- **The mixed economy**: Sweden's distinctive mix of capitalism and planned economy.
- **Corporatism**: Sweden's established practice to let, for instance, the labour market organization negotiate agreements in areas where other countries would use legislation, such as minimum wage and conditions of employment.
- **Universal welfare state policies**: the idea of creating welfare programmes that include (and are sufficient for) a large majority of the population.
- **The Rehn–Meidner labour market model**: the notion that structural change should be accelerated through wages being set independently of a company's actual ability to pay (a wage policy which shows solidarity with low-paid workers) and that the labour force can be directed towards efficient companies by means of active employment policies.[21]

The exact content of the Swedish model will probably never be agreed upon. Some authors talk instead of a Nordic or a Scandinavian model. Ryner (2007) defines the Nordic model as consisting of six parts: (1) a highly 'decommodified' wage relation; (2) public commitment to employment-promoting policies; (3) welfare state universalism; (4) a large social service sector; (5) a relatively 'women-friendly' welfare state; and (6) class compromise between capital and labour. Sweden is often said to be a typical example of the Nordic model, and Belfrage (2008) describes Sweden as '*the* social democratic economy' (p. 278, italics in original). In a specific demographic context, Trydegård (2004) is representative, describing the Swedish model for elderly care as universal, extensive, equal and equitable.

Noting the fact that different scholars use different definitions, Cox

---

[21] Lindbeck (1998) also mentions the so-called EFO model, which, in the 1960s, complemented the Rehn–Meidner model through the idea that wages in the sector exposed to competition should follow a trend defined by the sum of price increases on the global market and the labour force's change in productivity; see Edgren et al. (1973).

(2004) suggests that the most distinctive characteristic of the Scandinavian model today is the stickiness of its reputation, rather than the institutions and policies that make up the model. More striking than the varying ways in which the Swedish model has been defined, is that when different parts of the Swedish model are studied more closely, it becomes evident that several of them are ill-defined, not unique to Sweden, or that theory and practice diverge significantly.

The Mixed Economy

All economies that are not completely centrally planned, or pure market economies free from any state intervention, are mixed economies. Still, for a long period of time Sweden distinguished itself by incorporating far more features of a planned economy than most mixed economies in the West. Unlike many other countries, Sweden did not, for instance, phase out rent control after the Second World War. Rents more or less remained frozen from 1945 until 1975, and when rents were set, the norm was to have collective negotiations between the tenants and landlords. The rent control largely remains still today.

The capital market was regulated after the Second World War in order to be able to direct investments into socially prioritized areas, such as housing construction, which, due to rent control, did not attract capital on its own accord. Banks, insurance companies and pension funds were forced to put resources into housing bonds. The currency regulation meant that special permits were required for overseas capital transactions. The government oversaw all trade with foreign currencies through so-called currency banks, which were regulated according to a specific set of laws.

From 1955 the state directed company investments with the aim of stabilizing business cycles. Profits set aside for the so-called investment funds tax were made deductible. In order to use these funded resources, permission from the state was required, which in turn would be dependent on the labour market situation and other specific circumstances. The rules regarding investment funds remained until the tax reform of 1991.

Within the agricultural sector, tariffs and subsidies were used to enable farmers to live off farming and ensure that Sweden would be self-sufficient in the event of war. Prices were set in party negotiations between the state and agricultural interest organizations. The food industry also became subject to cartelization and a virtual monopoly was gained over the output of certain sectors (such as the sugar sector).

While regulations and subsidies (especially in the agricultural sector) were not unique for Sweden, they were a lot more extensive in Sweden compared to other countries. One way of illustrating the low degree of market economy in the Swedish mixed economy is to study the index of economic freedom which was developed by the Fraser Institute. The index quantifies economic freedom by equally averaging factors such as taxes, publicly owned companies, the judicial system, monetary system, free trade and regulations, resulting in a total score. According to this measure, Sweden ranked low in economic freedom and even substantially lower than several other Nordic countries. However, around the early 1980s, this situation would change: the degree of economic freedom increased in several countries, but in relative terms it increased much faster in Sweden than anywhere else – see Chapter 3.

Corporatism

Simply put, corporatism is the idea that the policies should be shaped by means of negotiations between the interest groups concerned, or between interest groups and politicians working closely together. When workers' insurance was first introduced in Sweden in 1901, the committee of the workers' insurance council included representatives from both the workers and the employers. In the 1930s, the model was expanded and applied to additional government institutions, where the Swedish trade union confederation (LO) and the employers' association (SAF) in particular were represented on various committees.

By being present and participating in official reviews and acting as bodies of referral, these organizations had a considerable degree of influence in policy-making. In practice, decisions were often made behind closed doors at Harpsund[22] in negotiations between the government and the relevant interest organizations, rather than in the Swedish parliament (Riksdagen). This type of model, where organizations are closely involved in the political process, is called corporatism. Corporatism is, for instance, the reason why Sweden does not have a legislated minimum wage. Instead, this issue is regulated in the collective bargaining agreements between the major labour market organizations.[23] For many high-income earners, these agreements also include topping up of income security in the social insurance systems.[24]

---

[22] Harpsund is a manor house in Flen Municipality, which since 1953 has been used as a country residence for the Prime Minister of Sweden.

[23] Skedinger (2005) shows that Swedish minimum wages often amount to 60–70 per cent of the median wage in the manufacturing industry, which sets the minimum wage at a high level compared to other countries.

[24] Ståhlberg (2003), Sjögren Lindquist and Wadensjö (2005, 2011).

Swedish corporatism is often described as something desirable using terminology such as 'interest articulation', 'interest aggregation' and 'expertise' (see Elvander, 1972). Elvander argues that the influence that the organizations had in policy-making was not a result of agitation or aggression, but rather a result of matter-of-factness and the extent to which the organization could be of use to the decision-makers. According to this view, the organizations viewed themselves as acting in the best interest of the public.

Corporatism is no longer as prevalent in Sweden. In the 1970s, the trade unions pushed legislation in several areas which previously had been regulated by the labour market organizations. Another example concerns organizational representation on committees and boards: in 1984 the Swedish trade union confederation (LO) had 1164 representatives on a total of 664 boards and committees which, in addition, also accommodated representatives from the employers' associations, the Swedish Farmers' Union (LRF) and other trade unions.[25] Since then, however, corporatism appears to have diminished in importance and the central wage negotiations between the Swedish trade union confederation and the employers' association became increasingly complicated. In 1992, the employers' organization, SAF, unilaterally left all boards and committees on which they previously had been represented. At times this event has been described as the end of the Swedish model.

Universal Welfare State Policies

Many attempts have been made to define and classify different types of welfare policies, and there is no doubt that Sweden, Norway, Finland, and to some extent also Denmark, have a specific type of welfare state where all major welfare programmes are constructed to include the middle classes. As shown by Bergh (2004), the labels 'universal', 'general', 'institutional', 'Scandinavian' and 'social democratic' welfare state are used in the literature to describe roughly the same thing.

A distinction often made is the one between general/universal and targeted/selective welfare programmes. The idea is that universal policies include the entire population whereas targeted programmes are directed towards specific groups. But the distinction is not obvious. For example, the rules surrounding housing allowance and social assistance, both often said to be selective programmes, are not less general than those governing pensions or study allowances: all of them list certain requirements which must be met in order for a citizen to receive support from the state.

[25] Rothstein (1992).

In order to make the distinction more meaningful it is helpful to distinguish between income selectivity and group selectivity. Child allowance in Sweden is not income tested, but still selectively aimed at families with children. Social allowance, on the other hand, is available to all citizens, but selectively aimed at those with low incomes and no assets.

Obviously, neither the Swedish welfare state nor any other welfare state is completely universal: Sweden also provides support and allowances aimed at low-income earners and certain other specific groups. But Sweden differs from many other countries in that both welfare services and social insurance benefits typically are sufficient to cover the demand for a broad majority of all households. In fact, many welfare state programmes in Sweden are particularly beneficial for the middle class: in Sweden, those with the lowest incomes are dependent on means testing for income support, and are, through their weak connection to the labour market, often excluded from income-related compensation found in for instance health and unemployment insurance. High-income earners have higher marginal tax due to the central government income tax, while at the same time the upper ceilings of compensation in terms of income support decrease their income security. Many low-income earners are excluded because they have not held a job long enough to qualify for income-related benefits, and high-income earners are affected by upper benefit limits, while still contributing by paying relatively high marginal taxes (Bergh, 2007). Even this, however, is not unique to Sweden. Rather, it is a result of the political logic behind welfare policy, as the middle class vote is imperative to politicians, as described by Goodin and Le Grand (1987).

Another feature which is argued to characterize Swedish welfare policy is the preventive social policy, that is offsetting problems at an early stage which would be difficult to solve later in life. Esping-Andersen (1994) argues that substantial public spending in the areas of employment, retraining, education and prevention of illnesses and accidents have led to smaller class differences, high levels of employment and a reduction of poverty. It is worth noting, however, that Sweden's internationally high level of public expenditure is explained largely by transfer payments – social insurance and pensions – rather than exceptionally high public consumption in areas such as health care, provision of general care and education. The transfer payments increased in particular during the 1970s: in 1965 they took up 25 per cent of Swedish public expenditure. In 1980 the same figure had risen to 80 per cent.[26]

---

[26] Schön (2000).

The Rehn–Meidner Model

Arguably, it is in the area of employment policies that it is most relevant to speak of a Swedish model. In this area the Swedish model typically refers to the Rehn–Meidner model for wage setting and industrial policy. Rynér (2002, p. 62) describes it as an 'overall concept of socio-economic regulation and governance'. The model is usually said to have been introduced at the LO congress in 1951, and is typically described as a coherent programme consisting of the following four parts:[27]

1. Combating inflation by keeping public expenditure low in order to prevent increasing demand to cause rising prices.
2. The solidaric wage-policy, based on the idea of equal pay for equal work, preventing less profitable businesses from staying competitive by lowering wages (and also preventing wages from increasing in successful businesses). By avoiding flexible relative wages for the allocation of labour, the model achieves both a reduction in income disparities among workers, and also accelerates the closing-down of unprofitable companies.[28]
3. Active labour market policies to make it easier for workers made redundant from unprofitable companies to gain employment in successful companies.
4. Selective employment stimulation for companies who need to recruit.

There are important differences between the model in theory and the actual policies implemented. Erixon (2006) warns against over-interpreting the importance of the model for Sweden's economic development on the basis that it was never fully applied. According to Björklund (1982), the most significant difference is that the politicians were not able to keep financial policy tight enough. As a result, there were clear tendencies towards overheating during booms, as well as unpredictable inflation. In addition, far from all employment policy programmes and measures have encouraged geographic labour flexibility. Instead, Björklund notes, distributive aspects have clearly been important. He further points out that the Employment Protection Act (*Lagen om anställningsskydd*, LAS) weakened the incentives to change employer and increased employment

---

[27] It should, however, be noted that this standard description probably has come about as a reconstruction the fact. Toft (2003) points out that the document that actually was presented at the congress of 1951 was not authored by Rehn, and only contained a very rough outline of employment policy.
[28] Björklund (1982) points out that labour was understood to be unresponsive to relative wage differences, which were thus a poor means of allocating labour.

costs by making it more difficult to dismiss employees. The 'last hired, first fired' rule goes very much against the idea of promoting geographic flexibility in the labour market.

Finally, Björklund concludes that the implications of the solidaric wage policies have never been made precise, but that the wage policies nevertheless have been in line with the programme to the extent that less productive labour and less productive companies were driven out of the market due to competition. As a consequence a trend towards increasing unemployment among young people (16–24 year olds) could already be seen in 1965 and onwards, according to Björklund.[29]

In some dimensions, the Rehn–Meidner model had the intended effect of increasing productivity and it also most likely accelerated the urbanization of Sweden, since successful companies often were located in the bigger cities. In a market economy this would have led to higher wages in the cities and an increase in the demand for housing, resulting in higher rents. This would, in turn, have made it profitable to build the housing that people demanded. In Sweden, these market signals had more or less been squandered by the solidaric wage policy and rent control. To alleviate the housing shortage, the state eventually invested in the so-called 'million programmes', centrally planned rental housing areas on the outskirts of the big cities.[30]

Yet another outcome of the model was that the considerable profits made by lucrative businesses had to be handled through taxation and a regulation of the capital market with the purpose of promoting growth. For individual taxpayers, the main focus of the taxation was the progressive income tax. Companies were taxed according to different rules. As long as capital was kept within the company, taxation was low. The regulations regarding depreciation of capital were favourable and it was easy to accumulate revenue within the company. The idea was to stimulate companies to invest their earnings, but it also had the effect of locking-in capital that would otherwise be allocated to more profitable investments. The stock market became less important as a source of finance and it became more difficult for start-ups to attract capital. Sweden became a country with wealthy enterprises – but with very few wealthy entrepreneurs.

---

[29] Björklund had already noted these problems in 1982 but the extended economic boom of the 1980s made the problems appear to be solved. After the crisis of the early 1990s the structural problems on the labour market again became visible, and still are so today – as discussed further in Chapter 6.

[30] The term 'the million programme' is usually attributed to a decision taken in the Swedish parliament in 1964 regarding the building of one million flats during the period 1965–74. Examples include Tensta and Rinkeby in Stockholm, Hammarkullen in Gothenburg as well as Rosengård and Hyllie in Malmö.

Opinions differ regarding the relevance of the Rehn–Meidner model today. The model was obviously built on the premise that the future belonged to the established large-scale enterprises, as Erixon (2004) puts it. Because common advantages of large-scale production can make it difficult for small companies to compete with large companies, the solidaric wage policy in practice becomes an entry barrier which protects the large-scale enterprises from competitive newcomers. It can also be questioned how government bureaucrats can possibly attain sufficient information to be able to assess which investments would be most profitable and thus at what selective employment stimulants should be aimed.[31]

One interpretation is that the model still, despite its inadequacies, served its purpose in Sweden during industrialism, when it was important to make use of the benefits that come from having economies of scale in the manufacturing industry. However, the Rehn–Meidner model is possibly less suited for a post-industrial society.

SUMMARY: SWEDEN AS THE CAPITALIST WELFARE STATE

In all, a full understanding of Swedish growth requires that standard explanations such as education, infrastructure, natural resources, the class compromise between capital and labour and the absence of war be complemented by institutional factors. The standard description of Sweden and the Swedish model captures many important aspects of Sweden. Yet it does not fully explain how Sweden became both prosperous and relatively egalitarian, two of the arguably most striking features about Sweden compared to other countries. Naturally, when describing a particular Swedish model, explanations will by definition focus on Swedish exceptionalism. Indeed, there are dimensions in which Sweden has been (and to some extent still is) exceptional, for example labour movement organization and welfare state universality. Focusing on the content of the Swedish model, however, means that we risk missing out on some explanations. The arguments presented in this chapter suggest that the origins of Sweden's economic success are less exceptional: just like most countries, Sweden grew rich because of well-functioning capitalist institutions. Sweden's period of high and sustained growth started with the introduction of property rights, free trade and non-corrupt meritocratic government. Recent findings in institutional economics strongly suggest that this was no coincidence.

---

[31] Both these arguments are put forth by, for example, Jakobsson (2004).

When it comes to explaining the compressed Swedish income distribution, the Swedish model again holds parts of the answer. For example, the high levels of union organization and the centralized wage structure clearly played a significant part in the increase in income equality. But the standard explanations must be complemented with factors such as land reforms and school reforms.

As the summary above implies, the common understanding of what the Swedish model constitutes is not sufficient to explain how Sweden became prosperous and egalitarian. This is not to suggest that the 'Swedish model' is an uninteresting concept. Nonetheless, by thinking of Sweden as a capitalist welfare state, we can gain a better understanding of Swedish success in terms of economic growth and equality. Early on, institutions which allow for a well-functioning capitalist economy had already been set up in Sweden. These were combined with welfare institutions which reduced poverty, increased literacy and spread out risks across the whole population. Several factors are liable to explain both economic growth and equality, such as the reformation of compulsory schooling, and the opportunities created by the land reforms in agriculture.

An even distribution of resources such as land and human capital predictably leads to an outcome that is more egalitarian than would have been otherwise. From an economic perspective, this method of creating equality has clear benefits compared to strongly progressive taxation and redistributive benefits, which tend to render work, effort, saving and education less worthwhile.

In bullet points, the capitalist welfare state can be described as follows:

- clear, stable and generally accepted private property rights;
- a predictable and non-corrupt state authority;
- a stable currency and functional financial markets;
- freedom of enterprise and free trade;
- well-adapted infrastructure;
- equality in the distribution of production resources;
- social insurance that spreads risks without significantly weakening work incentives;
- consensus and rationality in political decision-making.

It is of course not wrong to maintain that Sweden became wealthy through free trade and export-led growth. However, these factors would not have achieved the same positive result without a number of fundamental institutions, such as unambiguous property rights, a functional credit market and stable monetary policy.

The issue of how and why Sweden became egalitarian is not as widely researched as the issue of economic growth. However, much points towards the elementary school reform of 1842 and the nine-year compulsory school reform that took place approximately 100 years later playing a significant role, as did the early trade union movement, the increase in union membership during, above all, the first half of the twentieth century, centralized wage bargaining and a number of early social insurance reforms around the turn of the century. These include health insurance funds, occupational injury insurance and the state pension – but also reforms which took place later, such as the introduction of national and compulsory health insurance in 1955. It should be noted that none of these reforms demand particularly high taxes: Sweden's total tax burden was actually lower than, or equivalent to, that of the US up until 1960.

A number of factors have almost certainly contributed to both equality and growth. The land reforms, women's right of inheritance and the abolition of the guild system were all reforms which improved equality through enabling more people to participate on equal terms in the market economy – but they were also valuable in terms of economic activity and division of labour. The same is true regarding the extent of the judicial state and predictability of state behaviour: arbitrary and unpredictable state behaviour hardly benefits society's weakest.

When you think about Sweden as a successful capitalist welfare state where incentives for work and innovation were combined with institutions that promoted equality, it is easier to understand why things started to go downhill for Sweden after 1970. Sweden not only continued as a welfare state, but the welfare state was also expanded. However, the stable rules of the game that previously had led Swedish capitalism to become so successful were now replaced by interventionist policy-making, which almost rendered capitalism defunct.[32]

---

[32] As is shown further in Chapter 8, the development not only affected economic growth. Sweden also ran into problems with unemployment, which in particular affected those groups with a weaker position on the job market, such as immigrants and young people.

3. The 'not quite so golden' years 1970–1995

As a result of the strong economic growth which began in the mid-nineteenth century, Sweden had in 1970 become the fourth richest country in the world, after Switzerland, the United States and Luxemburg (measured as purchasing power-adjusted GDP per capita). Twenty-five years later, the gap between Sweden and the richest countries in the world was significantly wider. At its lowest, Sweden ranked 16th to 18th in the so-called welfare league, with some variation depending on source and method of calculation. Since then, Sweden has managed to narrow the gap to the top.

The ranking of countries in terms of average purchasing power should not be over-interpreted. First, Sweden was richer in 1995 than in 1970 – its fall in the ranking merely indicates that other countries have become even wealthier. Second, it is not very important if Sweden is the 15th richest or 20th richest country in the world, because there is so little separating rich Western countries that ranking becomes precarious. Sweden can these days be found in the group the OECD has termed 'High middle income group', which includes 14 countries.

Figure 3.1 shows the development of real GDP per capita in the United States, in 15 core EU countries and Sweden. It is easy to see that the period from 1970 to 1995 was not very good for Sweden.[1] From the mid-1990s and onwards, growth has been much higher.

While relatively little has been written about why Sweden became prosperous between 1870 and 1970, the problems that arose thereafter have been meticulously studied over and over again. Like all Western countries, Sweden was affected by escalating oil prices. However, the situation in Sweden was made worse by ill-advised economic policy. Swedish citizens noticed the problems in many different ways. For example, the Swedish Krona was worth much more abroad in 1970 than it was worth in 1995. At the beginning of the 1970s a German D-Mark could be bought for just

---

[1] At times, the lagging behind of Sweden has been questioned; see, for example, Korpi (1996) and the response by Henrekson (1996b). With the benefit of hindsight there is, however, not much to discuss. See also Henrekson (1999) for a summary of the debate.

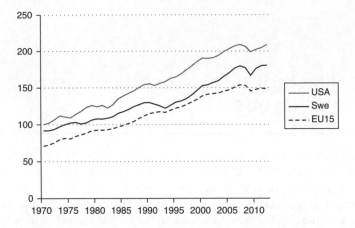

Note: The figure uses GDP per head in PPP dollars. Index 100 = USA 1970.

Source: OECD.

*Figure 3.1   Real GDP per capita 1970–2012 in the US, Sweden and the
            EU-15*

slightly more than one Krona. By the time the D-Mark was replaced by
the euro, the price had approximately multiplied by four.

   In a way, Sweden's failure to keep up is not wholly surprising. For
several reasons, it can be difficult for countries that are already among the
richest in the world to sustain strong economic growth. Other countries
can imitate wealthier countries' technology, learn from others' mistakes
and skip certain technological phases. In this respect, it is easier for poorer
countries to catch up with the richest, than it is for the richest countries to
keep on growing at a sustained pace. But the so-called catching-up effect
cannot explain why Sweden fell behind compared to, for instance, the
United States.

WHAT WENT WRONG?

Nowadays there is some agreement in the academic and political debate
that Sweden made a number of mistakes which led to an aggravation
of problems. The following description is an attempt to summarize the
consensus view.

   Looking closely at Figure 3.1, it can be seen that Sweden's lagging
behind becomes particularly evident during the recessions of 1976–78 and

1991–93. But the problems during these years are rooted further back in time. After the Second World War and up until the mid-1970s, Sweden pursued Keynesian stabilization policies, where the government aimed to manage household demand in order to minimize economic business cycle fluctuations. A well-known problem with such policies is that timing has to be very good in order for them to succeed. If the market is tightened too late during an economic boom, it will instead cause damage at the beginning of a recession. Expansionary measures during downturns may kick in too late and instead cause inflation and unsustainable consumption levels during the economic recovery. Further, active stabilization policies depend on unreliable economic forecasts, which provide estimates as to whether a downturn in the economy is temporary or the beginning of a longer recession. Finally, even if all these problems could somehow be solved, the active stabilization policies become increasingly less efficient when the economy is internationalized: employment in Sweden depends more on demand in other countries, and stimulating the demand in Sweden need not translate into higher employment in Sweden and becomes more dependent on the surrounding world.

From the mid-1970s onwards, Sweden began to subsidize problem-stricken industrial sectors and devalue the Swedish Krona in order to keep the industry competitive. These measures alleviated the situation in the short term, but the fundamental productivity and structural problems remained unsolved: too many actors in the Swedish economy essentially did the wrong things in the wrong way. Sectors and companies that were not competitive survived longer than they would have if they had been subjected to market conditions.

During the 1970s, real labour costs increased in an unsustainable manner, as labour productivity did not increase at the same rate. Costs increased mainly due to three reasons: taxes, labour market regulations and high nominal wage increases.[2]

- **Taxes**: in 1970 the payroll tax was 12.5 per cent of a salary. In 1979, it was 36.7 per cent. At the same time, the tax system became distinctly more progressive.
- **Labour market regulations**: many varied regulations were introduced during the 1970s: extended period of notice (1971); rules regarding construction workers having to be employed via instruction from the public employment office (1973); a responsibility to permit time off for and to pay for immigrants' Swedish language tuition (1973); protection against being fired on grounds of pregnancy (1974); law

[2] Source: Myhrman (1994, pp. 186–8).

on safety ombudsmen and safety committees (1974); limitations on
temporary employment (1974); law on permitting time off for trade
union activity (1974); law on permitting time off for education and
training (1975); obligation to inform the employment office of job
openings (1975); law on right of co-determination in the workplace
(1977); restrictions on overtime work as well as extended holiday
(the Annual Leave Act, 1978).[3]

- **High nominal wage increases**: in 1975–76, wage costs increased by
  over 40 per cent. It is sometimes argued that the centralized wage
  negotiations in Sweden contributed to a sense of responsibility
  (see for instance Lindgren, 2006), but as noted by Lindbeck (1998)
  increasing nominal wage costs of between 600 and 800 per cent in
  combination with repeated devaluations, is a rather clumsy way to
  achieve constant real wages after tax.[4]

The high marginal taxes meant that various forms of tax avoidance
became profitable, which prompted the Social Democrat and economist
Gunnar Myrdal (1978) to ask whether the Swedes had turned into a
'population of swindlers'.

High marginal taxes combined with unlimited deductions for interest
rate payments meant that loan-financed consumption became very cheap.
In addition, the inflation resulted in further lowering the real cost of debt
financing. In fact, as noted by Sandelin and Södersten (1978) a household
could take up a loan at 10 per cent nominal interest rate and deduct interest payments against a marginal tax of 60 per cent, thus decreasing the
nominal interest rate to 4 per cent. With inflation at 8 per cent, the real
interest rate became –4 per cent. If the house value increased at the same
rate as prices in general, people were in fact paid to live in a loan-financed
house. Naturally, debt financing became particularly attractive to high-
income earners with high marginal taxes, and the *actual* progressiveness
of the system was much lower than the high marginal tax rates would
imply.

In 1982, an offensive devaluation of the Krona, combined with the
international economic boom of the 1980s led many economic indicators
during the second half of the 1980s to appear very healthy. This made it

---

[3] Lindbeck (1998) interprets the many regulations as a result of the trade unions, during the
1970s, managing, via legislation, to push through terms and conditions which were not
reached in negotiations with the employers.

[4] It took a long time before Sweden could get the problem of high nominal wage increases
under control. According to the Swedish Central Bank, real wages increased barely half
a per cent per year during the 1975–95 period of high inflation, despite the nominal wage
increases averaging 8 per cent during the same period.

politically difficult to pursue a sufficiently tight fiscal policy, as described in great detail by Feldt (1991).

A number of political factors are also often said to have been important. The three-year terms of office, which were introduced with the election in 1970, contributed to short-termism in politics. Each government was hampered either by being newly appointed, or by an impending election. Also in 1970, a joint election day for the general-, county council- and local government elections was instituted, which led to the latter two being overshadowed by the general election. For local politicians the incentives to perform well in local politics were reduced and instead they hoped their mother-party would do well in national politics.

Another miscalculation concerning the constitutional reform of 1970 was the allocation of 350 seats – an even number – to parliament. Remarkably, in the 1973 election, the two opposing blocs won 175 seats each, and for three years, flipping a coin was the decision-making procedure of last resort. While Swedish political decision-making generally had been characterized by predictability and rationality, this was not the case for the so-called lottery parliament in place from 1973 until 1976.[5] The aim throughout the lottery-parliament of 1973–76 was to not let politics be determined by lot. However, a few of the cross-political agreements which were negotiated instead were associated with other problems. In the first so-called 'Haga agreement', the Social Democrats and the Liberal party reached a decision on lowering retirement age and income tax – financed by an increase in payroll tax. The propensity to raise those taxes not directly visible to employees has since been assiduously demonstrated in Sweden, and expanded on in, for example, Hansson (2006).

Simply put, the macroeconomic strategy from 1976 onwards was to use devaluations to postpone dealing with the fundamental economic problems. The strategy changed first when the effects of the offensive devaluation in 1982 died off at the end of the 1980s. At that point, the underlying problems regarding productivity, wage increases, household debt, and a rigid labour market contributed to deepening the crisis of the 1990s.

In the preceding chapter, it was shown how the stability created by certain capitalist institutions contributed to economic growth in Sweden. Taken as a whole, the policies pursued in the 1970s definitely did not result in stable rules. Legislation and tax rates were changed and added every

---

[5] Actual lottery-draws were, however, quite rare: during the parliamentary session 1975/1976, a mere 79 out of a total 1150 votes were decided by lot. Of these, the Socialist bloc won 39 times and the right-wing bloc won 40 times – all according to the Parliamentary Yearbook (*Riksdagens Årsbok*) 75/76.

year. Thus, in addition to policies now preventing or delaying necessary changes in Sweden, government behaviour had become less predictable.

The numerous devaluations created further disruptions. A fixed exchange rate that is regularly changed leads to speculation and uncertainty and hampers the ability of any economic actor to plan rationally. Additionally, the macroeconomic policies of the 1970s were unfortunate in that companies got into the habit of turning to government authorities for support and subsidies instead of being guided by actual productivity conditions and market demand.

WAS THE WELFARE STATE TO BLAME FOR SWEDEN LAGGING BEHIND?

Whether or not the welfare state is to blame for Sweden's lagging behind has been one of the core issues in the debate regarding Sweden's lagging behind. It should be clear from the summary above that many problems are more connected to failed macroeconomic policies than to failed welfare state policies. On the other hand, some have argued that generous welfare state benefits will affect social norms and lead to a weaker work ethic (Lindbeck et al., 1999), a view that seems to have some empirical support, as shown by Ljunge (2012). Studying sick leave benefits, Ljunge shows that those born in 1919 use sick leave benefits 45 per cent of the years they are in the labour force, whereas for those born in 1960, the take-up rate is almost 80 per cent. Given that rules have been constant and health has actually improved over the same time period, the findings suggest that social insurance programmes have long-run effects on behaviour.[6] Furthermore, studies of the relationship between total government size and economic growth in rich countries tend to find that total government size correlates with lower economic growth. This holds true also when controlling for the fact that automatic stabilizers such as unemployment benefits will increase government expenditure automatically during economic downturns.[7]

A possible interpretation is that the combination of unsuccessful

---

[6] See also Thoursie (2004) who showed that the number of men who reported sick increased as a result of sporting events on television.

[7] See the survey by Bergh and Henrekson (2011), who also note that it is conceptually problematic to discuss a causal effect from an aggregate such as government size on economic growth, and recommend analysing separately the mechanisms through which different taxes and expenditure affect growth. Not all taxes are equally harmful, and some studies identify public spending on education and public investment to be positively related to growth.

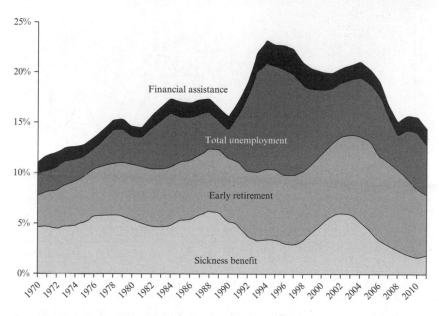

Source: Statistics Sweden.

Figure 3.2   *The share of the population aged 20–64 supported by various welfare benefits, 1970–2011 (full-time equivalents)*

macroeconomic policies and a generous welfare state with weak work incentives caused problems for Sweden. As an illustration, Figure 3.2 shows the share of the adult population supported by various welfare benefits from 1970 to 2011. It is crucial to achieve a balance between people who work and pay taxes, and people who do not. Clearly, the trend in Sweden from 1970 to 1995 was not sustainable: the share of adults not working more than doubled, from about 10 per cent to above 20 per cent after the crisis of the 1990s.

HOW DID SWEDEN MANAGE TO KEEP UNEMPLOYMENT LEVELS DOWN FOR SO LONG?

Another topic which has been the subject of much debate is Swedish employment and unemployment. When unemployment started to rise in the summer of 1990, it started from a very low level: open unemployment was less than 2 per cent, and had historically been much lower than in comparable countries (see Figure 3.3). How was it possible for Sweden

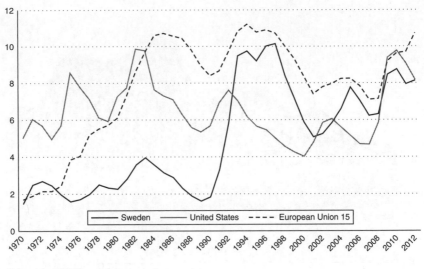

Source: OECD.

*Figure 3.3   Unemployment (age 15–64) in Sweden, the US and the EU-15
1970–2012*

to maintain such low levels of unemployment for so long, and why was
unemployment suddenly allowed to increase so dramatically?

Lindbeck (1998) discusses various possible reasons for Sweden's low
level of unemployment during the 1970s and 1980s, and arrives at two
important explanations:

- strong increase in public sector employment;
- recurring devaluations which sustained the competitiveness of the
  private sector.

Simply put, the expansion of the public sector led to the abolition of the
'housewife system', which was replaced by a system where child care and
elderly care is managed by the public sector. Rosen (1995) describes this
as Sweden, during the 1960s, 1970s and 1980s, nationalizing the family.

The development fostered gender equality as it became easier for
women to support themselves by earning their own income. Some who
are less enthusiastic about the development complain that the increased
taxes made it difficult to support a whole family on one income. From an
economic point of view there are clearly efficiency gains to be had from
daycare centers compared to each parent taking care of their own children

(that is, economies of scale in child care). These efficiency gains must, however, be large enough to offset the negative effects of raising taxes to subsidize child care.

Regarding the devaluations, they were, simply put, how Sweden lowered wages when Swedish industry was not doing too well. A market-based approach would have been to allow firms who are successful to pay their owners higher profits and their employees higher salaries, and to require unsuccessful firms to lower wages and profits. This way, market mechanisms would allocate labour and capital to the successful firms, forcing less successful firms out of business. Wage differences and large profits in successful firms function as important signals of where resources are most efficiently used.

The Swedish model can be explained as an attempt to achieve the same efficient resource allocation but without tolerating large wage differences. Instead of lowering wages in those companies and sectors which were not doing well, wages were brought down everywhere through devaluations, thus lowering the cost of goods from the Swedish export industry abroad. As a result, the important signal, indicating which firms and sectors were doing well and which were unsuccessful, was weakened.

When unemployment began to rise in the summer of 1990, there was agreement across the political blocs that wages should not be lowered through devaluations. At the same time, it was completely unthinkable that the trade unions would allow nominal wages to fall. As a result, there was a strong pressure on the least competitive firms to rationalize by decreasing their workforce. In Sweden, private demand fell considerably when a partially loan-financed wave of consumption passed into a period of household saving. Further, total tax revenue was already well above 50 per cent of GDP, and a continued expansion of the public sector was unthinkable for both the Social Democrat government in office and the Conservative government taking over. Consequently, unemployment increased dramatically, as uncompetitive firms dismissed personnel or went out of business.[8]

The ambition to avoid lowering wages through devaluing the currency, soon fell through. Despite tying the Swedish Krona to the European

---

[8] There were – and are – however a few divergent voices in the debate, according to whom future unemployment problems can also be solved by public sector expansion, financed by raised taxes, while simultaneously we accept that we become poorer through a dwindling exchange rate and rising inflation. This argument is best met by pondering the consequences of continuously solving unemployment problems with this strategy. What would happen if unemployment were always dealt with by public, tax-funded recruitment? What would happen if poor competitiveness was frequently compensated for by allowing the exchange rate to fall? Unless the aim is to turn Sweden into a poor, planned economy with a gigantic public sector, the strategy, sooner or later, has to be changed.

monetary system's currency ECU, which later became the euro, the Swedish Central Bank could no longer defend the fixed exchange rate, and in the autumn of 1992, the Krona was allowed to fall approximately 20 per cent relative to most other currencies.

Since then, Sweden has embarked on a new route: trying to achieve low unemployment without an endlessly growing public sector and without a falling exchange rate. Further, since the crisis of the 1990s there has been a trend towards public sector rationalization and increasing the number of jobs in the private sector. As the next chapter will show, this is not the only noteworthy change that has taken place in Sweden since the late 1980s.

SWEDEN AS THE INTERVENTIONIST WELFARE STATE

One way of understanding the problems which became apparent in Sweden from 1970 onwards is that Sweden, to a large extent, ceased being a successful capitalist welfare state. Instead, the state became increasingly interventionist: the rational separation of market and politics which characterizes the capitalist welfare state was replaced by a state that intervened in areas where good political intentions would run the risk of creating more problems than they solved.

The macro policies tried to stabilize business cycle fluctuations, but the fundamental imbalances contributed to making the crisis in the 1990s as severe as the depression in the 1930s. Concerning redistributive policies, the focus came to lie more on equality of outcome, which is obvious from the strongly progressive taxation. It is also explicitly clear from the opening paragraph of the 1980 Social Services Act, according to which the social services shall 'support people's financial and social security, equality in living conditions and active participation in social life' (my translation).[9] As a consequence, taxes and social benefits severely weakened the incentives to work, which hampered both the development of the economy as well as social equality.

Table 3.1 presents a simplified, contrasting description of the capitalist and the interventionist welfare state. It should be pointed out that the description compares two theoretical ideal types. Sweden has always been a mixture of these two extremes.[10] As a consequence, Sweden did not, in

[9] Socialtjänstlagen (SFS 1980:620).
[10] As an example, Jörnmark (2002) describes the Swedish business climate during the post-war period as ambiguous and contradictory. On the one hand, there existed an international market reasoning which paved the way for companies such as H&M and Ikea, while at the same time investment funds and public pension funds hampered domestic

Table 3.1   Outline contrasting the capitalist and the interventionist welfare state

	The capitalist welfare state	The interventionist welfare state
Relationship between market and politics	Rational division of labour	Politics superior to market
Macro- and stabilization policies	Stable rules of the game, focus on the supply side	Discretionary, active stabilization policies, demand management
Stance on property rights	Well-defined and well protected	Easily restricted through political decisions
Mobility of capital, goods and people	Free	Regulated
Preferred equality	Resource equality	Equality of outcome
Redistributive policies	Risk-spreading social insurance, tax financed welfare services (primary education and health care)	Progressive taxes, social policies, targeted subsidies

1970, shift from one extreme to the other. Many of the interventionist features had come into being much earlier than that and several of the capitalist features also remained throughout the 1970s. Nevertheless, the focal point of Swedish politics undoubtedly gradually moved during the golden years, from capitalism to interventionism, with interventionist policy-making peaking in the 1970s. However, as the next chapter will show, the tables have since turned again – and significantly so.

competition. In fact, competition was perceived by many as socially wasteful, according to Jörnmark: more than one company in each sector meant that production factors were duplicated, which seemed unnecessary and excessive! (ibid., p. 162).

4.   The return of the capitalist welfare state

During the last two decades of the twentieth century, Sweden changed so radically that it is difficult to do justice to all the changes on paper. Without a doubt, this was an eventful time across the world, but compared to other established Western democracies, the Swedish pace of change was still remarkable. This chapter summarizes the changes that took place. The Swedish reforms cover politics, economics and welfare policies, and it is difficult to distinguish which reforms have been more significant than others. In many cases it is not even possible to place the reforms in a clear chronological order, since they were under consideration for different durations of time before they finally were implemented. Appendix A contains an attempt to list the most significant changes chronologically, from allowing consumers to use answering machines from suppliers other than Swedish Telecom in 1980, to the introduction of the Swedish Telia shares in 2000. This chapter describes some of the most important reforms in more detail, and continues by asking if the changes represent the end for the Swedish model, and concludes that they should rather be seen as the return of the capitalist welfare state.

THE DEREGULATION OF THE CREDIT AND CURRENCY MARKET[1]

The legislation concerning credit policy measures was introduced in 1974. It entitled the government to grant the Central Bank permission to use a number of credit policy tools, such as liquidity requirements, minimum reserve requirements, lending regulation, general and specific mandatory investment and interest rate control. In practice, similar measures were used, together with a number of informal regulations as well as lobbying, during the entire period after the Second World War.

One of the purposes of the regulations was to avoid the banks being

---

[1] This section is primarily based on the political scientist Torsten Svensson's report for the Expert Committee for Public Finance Studies, Ds1996:37 and on Werin et al. (1993).

47

afflicted by liquidity crises. During the 1970s the regulations were also a means of providing for government borrowing, which during that period was steadily increasing.

As early as in the 1950s, different methods for evading the regulations had been developed, but it was not until the 1970s that the Central Bank started perceiving this as a serious problem. In 1980 a committee was set up to study credit policy and to suggest changes.[2] The committee concluded that regulations only have short-term effects. It was argued that a credit policy that utilized market-compliant measures was needed. Nevertheless, the committee maintained that some credit policy legislation should remain for emergency situations. Besides, a complete deregulation was perceived as unrealistic.

Even before the credit policy committee had concluded that liquidity requirements were inadequate for controlling the credit volume, the Central Bank's Board of Governors decided not to use liquidity requirements. The requirement was reintroduced at the beginning of 1983, only to disappear again in September the same year. The liquidity requirement was replaced by a ceiling on lending, which allowed the Central Bank's Board of Governors to decide by how much the banks were allowed to increase their lending compared to the year before. If the ceiling was exceeded, a penalty interest was levied, and as a last resort, the banks' borrowing in the Central Bank could be limited.

The gradual liberalization of the credit market continued with the economic-political proposal of 1984.[3] In 1985, interest rate control was completely removed after having been made a recommendation two years earlier. In November that same year, the lending ceiling was scrapped. With the intention of dampening the resulting credit expansion, non-interest-bearing cash reserve requirements for banks were increased from 1 to 3 per cent. But as noted by Englund (1999), monetary or fiscal policy did not change in any other way as a result of the deregulation. Banks, mortgage institutions, finance companies and others were now free to compete on the domestic credit market.

When the decision regarding deregulation was made, three main reasons were given. First, the need for lending regulations had decreased as a result of new treasury bills and financial markets which were created when the liquidity requirement was removed. Secondly, the rules had lost some of their effectiveness, and as State borrowing increased, there was a need for securities that could not be controlled by the means available to

[2] SOU (1982:52), A more efficient credit policy (*En effektivare kreditpolitik*).
[3] Proposition 1984/85:40, Guidelines for mid-term economic policies (*Riktlinjer för den ekonomiska politiken på medellång sikt*).

the Central Bank. Thirdly, and perhaps most importantly, the regulation had triggered a grey market that caused distortions in the credit market. Some of the large firms offered credit, and for those companies that were well connected, credit was easier to secure than for those that were not.

Internally, it was suggested that the objectives set out for the Central Bank were contradictory: industry investments were not to be hampered, but at the same time, the granting of credits was not to be overly expanded.

Currency control legislation was introduced at the beginning of the Second World War in 1939, and was at first only valid one year at a time. In 1959, however, the law was made permanent, which authorized the government to control or prohibit specific currency transactions. Up until 1974, currency regulation served an important role in the active stabilization policies, since it enabled strict control of both the inflow and outflow of capital.

The regulation was heavily debated, and in 1977 the newly appointed right-wing government appointed a committee to evaluate the regulation. The assessment was not complete until 1985, but an interim report was issued in 1980. In this report, a number of expert accounts were given, which unanimously concluded the currency regulation to be ineffective.

The final committee recommendation was to liberalize the currency market. The Conservatives were of the opinion that the regulation should be removed immediately, but the majority felt that currency regulation still had a role to play in stabilization policy. As a result, the compromise entailed a gradual removal of the currency regulation by the Central Bank. When the deregulation was completed in 1989, the Central Bank abolished the Exchange Control Act which stated that only the Central Bank was allowed to trade in foreign currencies.

It has been claimed that the removal of the lending ceiling on 21 November 1985 was done in a hurry and beyond democratic control. But in fact, the decision was in many ways typical of the Swedish style of policy making: the deregulations had been meticulously assessed well in advance and, what is more, the decisions to deregulate were arguably in line with the corporatist tradition in the sense that the actors involved were given a considerable amount of influence at the expense of parliament. Nevertheless, with the benefit of hindsight, it can be argued that some mistakes could have been avoided – as discussed further below.

THE TAX REFORMS

The Swedish tax system at the end of the 1970s is widely known for being highly progressive. Between 1977 and 1982, whenever a senior professional's income was increased, the tax rate at the margin was between 85 and 88 per cent. This was still merely income tax, and thus did not include payroll tax paid by the employer or value-added tax (VAT) on private consumption. If wealth tax was also included, the total marginal tax could exceed 100 per cent.[4]

Two major tax reforms have been carried out since then: one in the early 1980s (the so-called wonderful night's tax reform) supported by the Centre Party, the Liberals, and the Social Democrats, and one that was implemented in 1990 and 1991 (the so-called tax reform of the century) supported by the Social Democrats and the Liberals. The latter of the two reforms is the most comprehensive, but both are characterized by reducing progressivity while keeping total tax revenue high. In order to lower marginal taxes without decreasing total tax revenue, the tax base was broadened and consumption taxes increased. The idea was that the combination of lower tax rates and additional taxable activities would render the tax system more efficient. In 1987, government commissions were initiated regarding income tax, corporate taxes and consumption taxes.[5] The directives called for a tax system which lowered income taxes, reduced the progressiveness of the tax rate schedules, limited the possibilities for tax deduction, created greater coherence in capital taxation, and also encouraged private savings. In addition, the reform should be budget-neutral and not have any losers.

The reform passed by parliament (proposal 1989/90:110) concerned personal income taxation, corporate taxation, social security, value-added tax and selective consumption taxes. It was implemented in 1990 and 1991 and entailed broadening tax bases, reducing tax rates and shifting the emphasis from direct to indirect taxation. The idea was to create a more efficient tax system through lower tax wedges and a more uniform and equal taxation.

The changes that the tax reform entailed can largely be summarized as follows:

- The income tax was reduced for most people, and 85 per cent of wage earners would only pay income tax to the municipality, a roughly proportional tax at around 30 per cent (exact tax rate varied between municipalities). The remaining 15 per cent would also pay 20 per cent in national income tax, resulting in a top marginal income tax at around 50 per cent.

---

[4] Grosskopf and Rabe (1991). The situation was also observed by Swedish celebrity author Astrid Lindgren. After experiencing a total marginal taxation of 102 per cent, she wrote a satiric op-ed piece about a fantasy world called Monismanien, where a witch called Pomperipossa forced people to pay more in tax than they earned.

[5] SOU (1989:33–35) on tax reform.

- Fringe benefits would be taxed at their full market value.
- Capital income was to be taxed at 30 per cent, separately from employment income.
- The corporate tax was lowered from 52 to 30 per cent and the tax base was significantly widened.
- The base for value-added tax was extended to include most services and goods, and a standard tax rate of 25 per cent was introduced (an increase from the 23.46 per cent that was typically used before).
- Selective consumption taxes on, among other things, petrol and energy were increased, both to help finance the reform and to strengthen the environmental profile of the tax system.
- For distributive reasons, the basic deduction was increased for certain low-income intervals, and the child- and housing benefits were increased.

Since its introduction, the tax reform has been modified several times. The right-wing government lowered the corporate tax from 30 to 28 per cent, and in 1993 the principle of financing social insurance with ear-marked mandatory contributions was introduced. The contributions are tax deductible and should theoretically be tied to corresponding insurance benefits. The contributions were introduced at 0.95 per cent in 1993 and increased to 5.95 per cent in 1997. In 1998 the contributions were turned into pension contributions solely. In 2000 a system was introduced in which the wage earner is compensated for the general pension contribution through a specific tax break, and in 2007 an earned income tax credit was introduced, resulting in substantial changes compared to the tax reform.

Another departure from the principles of the tax reform came in 1995 when the national income tax was raised from 20 to 25 per cent, described as a temporary austerity tax. In 1999 the additional five percentage units were moved further up the income tax scale, which thereby acquired two brackets: in the lower bracket a national tax of 20 per cent is taken while in the upper bracket the tax is set at 25 per cent.

The share of taxpayers who pay national tax has most of the time been greater than the 15 per cent stated in the guidelines laid down by parliament at the time of the tax reform.[6] The reason for this is that real income

---

[6] The share has typically varied between 15 and 20 per cent of all income earners, or roughly one third of all full-time employees aged 20–64 (Skatteverket, 2012). Since its introduction, the top marginal tax rate of 57 per cent has applied to between 8 and 10 per cent of all full-time employees.

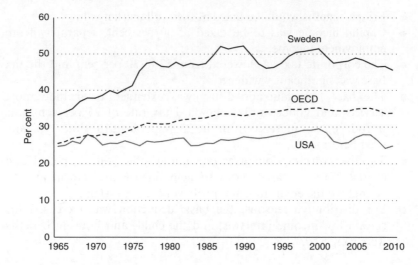

*Figure 4.1   Tax revenue as a share of GDP 1965–2010 in Sweden, OECD
             and the US*

growth has pushed more income earners above the threshold, clearly a
politically convenient way to raise taxes.

Despite all the deviations, the tax reform still means that Sweden
has moved away from strongly progressive taxation. Before the tax
credits were introduced in 2007 and beyond, Sweden was very close to
a proportional tax system. Apart from the national income tax, Sweden
would essentially have a so-called flat-rate tax – that is, a system where
marginal tax above the basic allowance does not increase with income.
The introduction of earned income tax credits in 2007–10 increased progressivity substantially in low-income intervals, by lowering the average
tax rate more for low-income earners than for medium and high-income
earners – a consequence of the amount by which income tax is lowered
being bounded from above.

Figure 4.1 illustrates the tax revenue as a share of GDP in Sweden, the
EU-15 and the OECD. The Swedish tax share is on average 10 percentage units higher than the EU-15 average and 14 percentage units higher
than in the OECD. As is evident in Figure 4.2, the structure of income
tax changed considerably more than the average tax burden, as a result
of the reform. From the top levels, the marginal tax has decreased, partly
during the 1980s but, above all, in 1991 as a result of the tax reform in
1990.

As shown in Table 4.1, the main structure of tax revenue has not

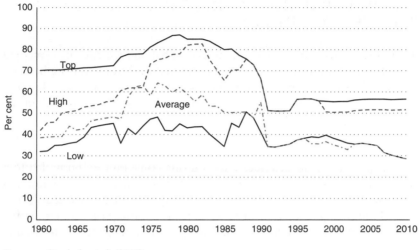

Source: Stenkula et al. (2013).

Figure 4.2 *Marginal income taxes 1960–2010, for low, average, high income earners and top rate*

Table 4.1 *The distribution of tax revenue 2003 and 2011 (% of GDP)*

	2003	2011
National income tax	1.3	1.4
Local income tax	16.5	15.4
Insurance contributions and payroll taxes	15.8	14.8
VAT	9.3	9.5
Excise taxes	4.2	3.6
Tax credits	−2.3	−5.4
Real estate tax	1.0	0.4
Corporate income tax	2.1	3.2
Wealth tax	0.4	abolished
Misc.	2.3	1.7
Total	50.6	44.6

Source: Skatteverket (2004, 2012).

changed very much since 2003: the largest revenue sources for the public sector are the local income tax, VAT and the payroll taxes. These are all almost entirely proportional. The progressive elements, such as wealth tax and national income tax, constitute a very small share of the tax revenue.

TAX REFORM AND CREDIT DEREGULATION IN THE WRONG ORDER?

With the benefit of hindsight, considerable agreement has emerged that the credit deregulation fuelled a speculation bubble on the housing market. To some extent, the problems became particularly severe because the credit deregulation took place before the tax reform, rather than the opposite way round.

As mentioned above, tax-deductible interest rate expenses combined with high marginal taxes and high inflation made loan-financed consumption beneficial for households. The resulting consumption boom led to a dramatic increase in house prices. When the marginal taxes were lowered and inflation decreased, the benefits of loan financing decreased, and household savings turned from negative (that is, households accumulating debts) to positive. Demand for housing decreased and prices started falling very rapidly.

Many argue that it would have been better if the 1990 tax reform had been implemented before the credit deregulation. It is most likely that it still would not have eliminated all the problems. Sweden was not the only country to deregulate the credit and currency markets, and the immediate outcomes were similar in most countries: increased lending overheating and financial crisis (Kask, 1997). Among the Nordic countries, Denmark managed the deregulation best, probably because it was initiated early on and thereby avoided the strong increase in lending which then took place in Norway, Sweden and Finland.

The tax reform of 1990 has been assessed by a public commission.[7] It was concluded that the tax reform had been necessary, that it contributed to lowering the distortionary costs of taxation and that the redistributive policy objectives largely had been met even though high-income earners had profited somewhat more than intended. The financial forecasts, however, had been too optimistic. The idea was to finance income tax reductions with broader and slightly higher consumption taxes (mainly VAT). The forecasts did not take into account that the revenue from consumption taxes before the reform was abnormally high because household consumption was unsustainably high, fuelled both by the economic boom of the 1980s and increasing debts after the credit deregulation. As a result, when household savings increased, which fundamentally was a desired outcome, the result was a decrease in revenue from consumption taxes. The insufficient financing of the tax reform contributed significantly to the budget deficit during the early 1990s.

[7] SOU (1995:104).

CENTRAL BANK INDEPENDENCE AND PRICE STABILITY

Since January 1993 the Swedish Central Bank has been working towards the goal of keeping inflation, as measured by the yearly increase in the consumer price index, at 2 per cent, with an error margin of 1 percentage unit either way (though the 2 per cent goal has never actually been legislated). After the credit market deregulation, the government assigned a committee to consider various goals and management forms for the Central Bank. Later, the right-wing government issued a supplementary directive which assigned the committee the added task of assessing the consequences for the Swedish Central Bank of the plans for a European monetary union, as well as how the Central Bank could be made more independent.

The commission report was presented in the spring of 1993.[8] It concluded, among other things, that in the early 1990s the Central Bank was already de facto relatively independent. For example, the Governor of the Central Bank, Bengt Dennis, remained in his position when the right-wing parties won the election in 1991. However, for monetary policy to be effective in the long run, the commission wanted to increase credibility by making the Central Bank independent in a legal sense as well. The suggestion was to legislate a goal for price stability, though not for the inflation rate.

Nevertheless, by late summer 1992 the Central Bank had already informally investigated alternative assignments for the bank in the event that the Swedish Krona would be allowed to float. According to Andersson (2003) one of the alternatives was to set an inflation goal, which is also what the Central Bank chose to do. Thus, the committee proposals were put to practice even before they had been published.

Interestingly, the Central Bank committee proposals did not result in any bill from the right-wing government, since there was no support from the opposition and the established norm was that such constitutional changes needed broad political support. Later, when Erik Åsbrink, the Deputy Minister of Finance in 1990 who at that time initiated the Central Bank commission, became Minister of Finance in 1996, he also became chairman of a working group involving representatives from all parliamentary parties. The work resulted in a proposal, in which it again was concluded that the Central Bank essentially is independent.[9] In order to increase credibility as well as out of consideration for the EU, the proposal

---

[8] SOU (1993:20), The central bank and price stability [*Riksbanken och prisstabiliteten*].
[9] Prop. 1997/98:40, The status of the Swedish Central Bank [*Riksbankens ställning*].

still put forward that the Central Bank independence be established by law, which would take effect on 1 January 1999. This also meant that the price stability objective was eventually established by law.

SOCIAL INSURANCE REFORMS[10]

During the 1980s, the debate concerning the weak work incentives and moral hazard problems in the social insurance systems intensified. Among other things it was highlighted that the combined effect of social insurance compensation levels at 90 per cent and topping up contracts negotiated by the unions and employer organizations meant that large groups received almost full wages when they were on sick leave. This was changed during the 1990s.

In March 1991 the level of compensation for sickness benefit was lowered, after having been kept at 90 per cent since 1974.[11] The new levels were set at 65 per cent for the first three days of compensation, 80 per cent from the fourth day onwards, and 90 per cent commencing on the 91st day of the compensation period. In April 1993 a qualifying day without compensation was introduced into the sickness benefit insurance.

The levels of compensation in the unemployment benefit were changed from 90 to 80 per cent in 1993 and further lowered to 75 per cent in 1996. In autumn 1997, the level of compensation was again set at 80 per cent. For unemployment benefit, the upper compensation ceiling is significantly lower than it is for sickness benefit, and during the 1990s the number of wage earners with incomes above the ceiling increased from approximately 45 per cent in 1992 to 50 per cent in 1997. However, the lowest level of compensation increased somewhat during the 1990s.

The parental benefit was also changed from 90 to 80 per cent of income during the 1990s. The same reduction has affected the temporary parental allowance when caring for a sick child, which nevertheless does not include a qualifying day such as that which was introduced for regular sick pay.

---

[10] The following section is based on the Swedish Ministry of Health and Social Affairs (2002) and the Social Insurance Office's own compilation of regulation changes concerning social insurance.

[11] The reduction also included maternity allowance, allowance for next of kin, disease-carrier allowance, occupational injury allowance and sick pay within the so-called period of coordination according to the law on occupational injury insurance.

THE PENSION REFORM

The widely encompassing Swedish pensions reform can be traced back to the pensions committee appointed in 1984 to study the need for changes in the pensions system. The committee worked for six years and by 1990 it had become clear to them that the system in place (the ATP system introduced in 1960 after the referendum in 1957) was fraught with such considerable problems that a reform would be preferable.[12] In 1991, the right-wing government appointed a working group for the reform process. According to the directive, the new system had to be financially sustainable, increase long-run saving and encourage people to work.

The committee report was presented in 1994 and resulted in a government bill with guidelines that the pensions system should be public, compulsory and based on the life cycle principle, that is a person's pension should correspond to the fees paid throughout life.[13] The fees were set at 18.5 per cent of pensionable income (very close to taxable income before tax). Only incomes below an upper ceiling are pensionable, but the ceiling is indexed.[14] An implementation group, with representatives from the Social Democrats, the right-wing parties as well as experts on the subject, put forward the final proposal and the starting date was set at 1 January, 1999.

The new system combines a traditional pay-as-you go design with a fully funded part. Sixteen percentage units of the fees are used to pay today's pensioners, while simultaneously the same amount is set aside for the paying individual's own pension entitlement. The remaining 2.5 percentage units are set aside for the so-called premium pension, an individual, fully funded savings system. In 1997, the government set up a committee to study the funded part of the pension system.[15] The committee suggested that the premium pension should be a social insurance shaped as a private insurance, administered by a new authority, the Premium Pensions Authority (*Premiepensionsmyndigheten*).[16] Other important features of the new system include a guaranteed minimum pension for people who have had a low income, as well as an automatic balancing (the so-called brake) of the system in order to adjust pension expenditure to economic and demographic fluctuations.

[12] SOU (1990:76), Public pension [*Allmän pension*].
[13] SOU (1994:20), Reformed Pension System [*Reformerat pensionssystem*].
[14] Technically, yearly incomes below a threshold of 7.5 basic amounts (426 750 SEK in 2014) increase individual pension rights.
[15] SOU (1997:131), Law on premium pension [*Lag om premiepension*].
[16] This government agency existed only from 1998 to 2009. In 2010, a unified pension agency was started (*Pensionsmyndigheten*).

Once every year, each citizen born in or after 1938 receives an envelope containing information on accrued pension rights so far, as well as a prognosis of the future pension level depending on the age of retirement.

DECENTRALIZATION AND ORGANIZATIONAL EXPERIMENTATION

Despite the fact that a large part of the Swedish welfare state's resources are spent at municipal or local level, the degree of local government autonomy has for a long time been comparatively low. In many cases, the local governments are required to fulfil the tasks that are laid down in parliament through target decisions. Further, a remarkably complex balancing system makes it difficult in practice for the municipalities to influence their own economy.

However, the new municipal law of 1992 strongly increased the local governments' ability to shape their internal organization independently. In 1993 the government subsidies allocated to the municipalities changed from being earmarked to general subsidies. At the same time, the local governments' areas of responsibility had increased through the decentralization of schools in 1991, and the trend continued with the elder care reform of 1992 (the so-called ädel-reform), which gave the municipalities responsibility over old age people with their medical treatment completed. Yet another example is the mental health care reform in the mid-1990s. Municipalities also became more active in labour market policies, not so much as a result of a deliberate decentralization but as a consequence of being financially responsible for the social assistance to people who do not qualify for unemployment insurance.[17] Hence, throughout the 1990s, local governments were given and took more responsibility for public welfare provision.

Increased independence and responsibility led local authorities to experiment with new organizational and management forms. Some prefer to bundle these changes under the label 'New Public Management' (NPM), but as argued by Lantto (2001), general statements regarding all reforms included in the NPM label are not tenable. Instead, the effects of reforms such as government by objective, contracting out and voucher systems must be separately assessed. Sometimes a prospective payment system (PPS) and Diagnosis-related group (DRG) in health care is also included under the NPM label. DRG is a system to classify hospital cases into meaningful groups that can be used to monitor resource use and measure

---

[17] Ministry of Health and Social Affairs (2002).

productivity. Sweden was quick to start using the system as early as 1986 (Calltorp, 2008).

When the local government legislation no longer regulated every detail of how councils should be organized, different variations on the so-called buyer–producer model could be tested. The principle behind the model holds that politicians, on behalf of the citizens, order or 'buy' the service, which then is produced by the administration or procured on the market. The motives for using this organizational form have included both the possibilities for streamlining as well as flexibility. The model gained ground in the beginning of the 1990s but interest has since dwindled.[18]

CONSUMER CHOICE AND VOUCHER SYSTEMS

During the 1990s, the organization of the publicly financed consumption of welfare services was radically transformed. Carl Bildt's government declaration in 1991 introduced a 'freedom of choice-revolution' in welfare policies. This referred to how tax-financed welfare production did not necessarily have to be produced by the public sector. Instead, the government would manage the monitoring and financing side, and private and public producers would compete for production. This would create opportunities for freedom of choice, diversity and more efficient use of tax money.

The following year, a school voucher system was introduced, according to which the local authorities were instructed to pay independent schools at least 85 per cent of the municipal schools' average cost per student. The independent schools, however, were not allowed to charge any student fees and they had to be recognized by the National Agency for Education, that is they needed to comply with the Education Act and follow the national curriculum.

Since private schools previously had secured financing by charging substantial fees, it was hoped that the school voucher reform would stimulate socio-economic diversity also in independent schools.[19] Giving students the right to use the school voucher across the municipal border, while the home municipality still had to pay, further extended the reform.

When the Social Democrats took over office in the autumn of 1994, only minor modifications were made to the reform: the 85 per cent requirement was changed to at least 75 per cent, supported by a commission

---

[18] See Karin Svedberg Nilsson's contribution in SOU (2000:38). See also Montin and Wikström (2002).

[19] Prop. 1991/92:95 on freedom of choice and independent schools (*om valfrihet och fristående skolor*).

which maintained that compensation above 75 per cent distorted competition.[20] It was later also established that an independent school should not be approved if it has noticeably negative consequences for the educational system in the municipality in which it is located. For a long time, the debate regarding school vouchers primarily concerned the extent to which religious independent schools should be allowed within the system. As a result of increasing evidence of quality differences between schools and of school results worsening, the debate intensified – as is discussed further in Chapter 6.

Although the school voucher is probably the most well-known voucher system, it was not the first. As early as 1985, Nacka municipality (close to Stockholm) instituted a 'foot care voucher' for pensioners. Danderyd, another municipality close to Stockholm, pioneered contracting out of elderly care in 1989 through an agreement with Svensk Hemservice (presently Attendo).

The private production of tax-financed welfare services has increased slowly but steadily since these first steps.[21] In 2012, private providers' share of total cost was about 15 per cent. For primary schools, the share of students has increased from a few per cent in the early 1990s to 12 per cent in 2010. For secondary schools (gymnasium) the trend has been steeper since 2000, exceeding 25 per cent in 2011. For child care, the share of children with private providers reached 20 per cent in 2012, up from 15 per cent in 2000. For elder care, both old people's homes and home-help services reached 20 per cent in 2011, the trend being slightly steeper for home-help services. For primary care, private providers' cost share exceeded 30 per cent in 2011, but the cost share for privately provided specialized health care has barely increased at all, holding steady between 5 and 10 per cent. The share of private providers is probably highest for personal assistance according to the 1994 Act concerning support and service for persons with certain functional impairments (LSS, *Lagen om stöd och service till vissa funktionshindrade*), where 55 per cent of users in 2010 had used private providers.

SWEDEN JOINS THE EUROPEAN UNION

In the summer of 1990, Sweden applied for membership of the European Community (EC). The membership negotiations began in 1993. On 1 January 1994, the Agreement on the European Economic Area (EEA)

---

20 SOU (1992:38).
21 Jordahl (2013).

came into effect,[22] whereby the countries in the European Free Trade Association (EFTA) were granted access to the EC's internal market and its four freedoms: free movement of goods, services, capital and persons.[23] A few months later, the negotiations on Sweden's membership conditions were finalized. On 13 November 1994, the Swedes voted 'yes' to membership in a referendum and on 1 January 1995 Sweden became an EU member state.[24]

THE FOUR-YEAR OFFICE TERM

In 1967 a commission on the constitution proposed that the government term of office be shortened from four to three years, which was implemented starting with the election in 1970. Sweden nevertheless returned to four-year terms of office starting in 1994. This shift can be traced back to a debate on how the three-year office term had made political efforts somewhat erratic: it takes at least one year for a government to become familiar with the work, and when there is less than a year left until the election, it can be difficult to make long-term decisions in the best interest of the public. Therefore, a government who has a three-year term of office in practice only has one year in which it can fully concentrate on work, which is the term's middle year. Further, the official commission on the future of democracy pointed to an aggravation of budget work and that the system of government commission would have to work faster if sizeable reforms were to be carried out during an office term.[25] A term of office longer than four years was rejected by the commission on the grounds that interest in politics may diminish if terms are too lengthy.

REFORMING THE PARTY-LIST VOTING SYSTEM

Another issue brought to the fore in the official commission on the future of democracy was the possibility of voting for persons in addition to voting for parties. The reform means that voters may vote for a specific

[22] Prop. 1991/92:170, *Europeiska ekonomiska samarbetsområdet*.

[23] The one exception is Switzerland, who in a referendum voted against the EEA agreement. The EFTA was established in 1960 as a free trade association for European states unwilling to join the then European Economic Community (EEC) which has now become the EU.

[24] The result in the referendum was 52.3 per cent yes-votes and 46.8 no-votes (with 0.9 per cent blanks).

[25] SOU (1987:6), The conditions for democracy (*Folkstyrelsens villkor*).

candidate on the party list. The candidate who receives the most votes is elected first; the candidate with the second most votes is elected second, and so on. After a trial in 1994, the system was implemented fully in the 1995 European Parliament election and in the 1998 general elections. As the system was initially constructed, the number of personal votes is only significant if the candidate receives more than 8 per cent of the party's votes – if not, the party list's priority order is followed. The corresponding threshold for county- and local government election is 5 per cent. In 2010, the national 8 per cent barrier was lowered to 5 per cent, which applied for local elections.

An evaluation of the party list proportional representation system was carried out after the election in 1998. The commission concluded that effects were small, but if anything the reform had improved relations between voters and politicians, and had contributed to increased interest.[26] In 1998, almost one third of the voters cast personal votes. The share has since decreased, but increased again to 25 per cent in 2010.

THE NEW BUDGET PROCESS

Alongside the economic crisis of the early 1990s, two important documents highlighted the need for changes to the national budget process: a commission on public debt and the budgetary process, and the so-called Lindbeck Commission.[27] At the same time, a parliamentary review of the budget process was carried out.

The parliamentary committee produced a number of proposals, including switching from the fiscal year to the calendar year. More importantly, it was suggested that the budget proposal should be comprehensive when submitted: additional proposed expenditures put forward after submission would only be permitted in exceptional cases. Additionally, 27 expenditure areas were introduced. The government first draws up a framework for every expenditure area (excluding interest payments on public debt) and after committee drafting, the parliament decides on how the appropriations should be allocated among the different areas. Hence, within this system, budget proposals submitted by government and the opposition cover the entire budget. Any expenditure increases proposed later on require financing within the framework, that is, from a corresponding decrease in spending somewhere else. This arrangement was first applied to the 1997 fiscal year.

[26] SOU (1999:136).
[27] Ds 1992:126 and SOU (1993:16), respectively.

In the supplementary government proposal of 1995, it was suggested that a ceiling on spending be introduced with the purpose of restricting state expenditures, as continued tax increases were not deemed feasible. Moreover, economic policy would become more predictable and thereby encourage economic growth. The expenditure ceiling was initially also intended to apply to county councils and local governments, but with respect to municipal autonomy, a balanced budget was stipulated instead.

The ceiling is nominal and is set for three years at a time according to a rolling schedule, and includes a budgeting margin to cover market fluctuations. The parliament is not, however, bound by any law stipulating that the national budget must not exceed the expenditure ceiling.

LIBERALIZATION OF AGRICULTURAL POLICIES[28]

Up until the mid-1980s, agricultural policies were still based on the 1933 agreement between the Farmers Alliance (*Bondeförbundet*, presently the Centre Party) and the Social Democrats Party, where the Farmers Alliance supported spending to fight unemployment in exchange for agricultural price controls. The policies had three goals: autarchy in foods; protecting farmer incomes; and efficient structural transformation in agriculture (Hedlund and Lundahl, 1985). The combination of price controls, tariffs and subsidies rules and regulations continuously expanded to cover ever-increasing areas. The farming bureaucracy grew, both in terms of organization as well as number of employees. Powerful special interests emerged concurrently with the regulations and these special interests then took action to defend and further strengthen the existing regulations. According to Bolin et al. (1984), agricultural policy is a typical example of how well-organized groups have been influential in politics, a classic example of so-called rent seeking (Tullock, 1967).

A number of contributions to the debate as well as reports in the 1980s significantly altered the situation, by describing the consequences of the subsidies and regulations.[29] Lindberg (2007) attributes an important role to economists' analysis of the situation using public choice theory,

---

[28] The sources used for this chapter are Flygare and Isacson (2003) as well as Lindberg (2008).

[29] Important examples are Bolin et al. (1984), Hedlund and Lundahl (1985), an official commission on food prices and food quality (SOU 1987:44 Livsmedelspriser och livsmedelskvalitet) as well as a report from the unit for studies in public sector economics on food prices and food quality (Ds 1988:54 Alternativ i jordbrukspolitiken).

highlighting that agricultural policy was closely linked with industry interests and could perfectly well be explained as service to vested interest. Most obviously, the policies created a prominent waste of resources: food surpluses in Sweden (as well as in the rest of Europe and the United States) had no obvious market as the world market was filled with subsidized milk, meat, grain and other products.

When the Federation of Swedish Farmers (LRF, *Lantbrukarnas Riksförbund*) realized that there was a political majority in favour of reforms, they chose a constructive course of action to gain influence over them, rather than just saying 'no' and protesting against change.[30] The deregulation from 1 July 1991 entailed previously negotiated prices being replaced by market prices, but at the same time the Swedish Agricultural Administration was instituted to facilitate the adaptation to the deregulated market, and 14 billion SEK were set aside as compensation for adaptation.

Importantly, the deregulation was never fully implemented since Sweden's entry to the EU entailed a re-regulation of Swedish farming.

SUMMARY: THE DEATH OF THE SWEDISH MODEL?

How should the changes described above be characterized? From a superficial view it seemed for a long time as if very little had happened: taxes and total public spending remained high, and social expenditure actually increased slightly. But as noted by Blomqvist (2004), aggregate spending levels do not capture the fact that the organization of the welfare state has been very much transformed.

It is also clear that Sweden after the reforms is considered to be a competitive economy with a good business climate. In 2013, the Global Competitiveness Report[31] ranked Sweden number 6 out of 148 countries, the World Bank's Doing Business index[32] ranked Sweden 14 out of 189, and in the World Competitiveness Yearbook,[33] Sweden ranked 4 out of 60. Table 4.2 summarizes Sweden's strengths and weaknesses in these rankings.

The Index of Economic Freedom again provides a useful descriptive tool. The index quantifies the degree of economic freedom in five dimensions:

---

[30] Flygare and Isacson (2003, p. 252).
[31] Available at http://www.weforum.org/reports/global-competitiveness-report-2013-2014.
[32] Available at http://www.doingbusiness.org/rankings.
[33] Available at http://www.imd.org/wcc/.

Table 4.2   Positive and negative factors in the assessments of the Swedish business climate

Positive factors	Negative factors
Good supply of risk capital	Taxes, especially the high income taxes
Research and researchers, in particular natural scientists	High labour costs
Extensive Internet use	High level of cost in general
Efficiency in the legal system	Low labour market flexibility
Effective patents and intellectual property rights	Poor investor protection
Low customs tariffs	Extensive bureaucracy
Cooperation between the labour market organizations	Poor quality of taught mathematics
Low corruption	Lacking local competition
Stringent environmental requirements	Weak competition and anti-trust law
High quality of local suppliers	Few national purchases of advanced technical equipment
Cooperation between clusters	Lack of local suppliers
Good infrastructure	Highly-educated foreigners' opinion of the Swedish business climate
Female representation in politics	
Skilled labour	
Low corporate tax	

Source: Based on Wengström (2006),

1. size of government;
2. legal structure and security of property rights;
3. access to sound money;
4. freedom to trade internationally; and
5. regulation of credit, labour and business.

Each dimension consists of several components that are scored and weighed together, resulting in a score between 0 and 10 for each dimension. The aggregated economic freedom is the average of the score in the five dimensions (equally weighted).

As shown by Table 4.3, among the countries that most frequently appear in research on the welfare state, Sweden is one of the countries where aggregate economic freedom increased the most over a 20-year period.

Table 4.3 still does not do justice to the intensity of reform in Sweden. The reason is that Sweden increased economic freedom without substantial

Table 4.3   Top reformers (measured by increase in aggregate economic freedom over 20 years)

	1975–1995	1980–2000
New Zealand	3.0	2.1
United Kingdom	2.1	1.8
Sweden	2.0	1.9
Norway	2.0	1.6
Australia	1.9	1.2
Denmark	1.6	1.7
Netherlands	1.4	0.9
Finland	1.4	1.2
Italy	1.2	1.8
France	1.1	1.2
Canada	0.9	0.6
Germany	0.8	0.5
Switzerland	0.7	0.6
United States	0.6	0.6
Belgium	0.3	0.5

reductions in size of government. As a result, dimensions 2 to 5 have changed much more than dimension 1. The changes are described by Bergh and Erlingsson (2009) as liberalization without welfare state retrenchment. By excluding dimension 1, measuring government size, from the measure of economic freedom, Figure 4.3 shows economic freedom for dimensions 2 to 5 for the countries in Table 4.3. The countries have been categorized according to common practice in this type of research, defined as Scandinavian, Continental and Anglo-Saxon welfare states.[34] Sweden has kept a large public sector, high taxes and a universal welfare state – but still increased economic freedom considerably, through deregulation and liberalization.

The Anglo-Saxon model combines a small public sector with a high degree of economic freedom – which was high already in the 1970s. The Continental European welfare states have more extensive government but since the mid-1970s they have also had less economic freedom. The Scandinavian countries distinguish themselves by having high taxes *as well as* a very rapid increase in economic freedom. Among the Scandinavian countries, Sweden further sets itself apart by having even higher taxes than

---

[34] Other definitions are also common, for example social democratic, conservative and liberal welfare states. The division of welfare states into three categories is usually accredited to Esping-Andersen (1990), but can be traced back to Titmuss (1974). The categories are far from unproblematic – see Abrahamson (1999).

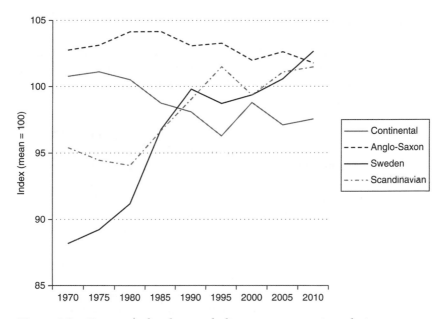

Figure 4.3 *Economic freedom excluding government size relative to mean 1970–2010*

the others, which explains why high taxes and costs in general appear as a negative factor in the Swedish business climate. Concerning the degree of economic freedom, Sweden starts from a low level in the 1970s and ends up with an above-average level in 2010.

There is still agreement on the Swedish welfare state having survived the crisis of the 1990s with most of its distinguishing features intact: despite organizational changes, the character and basic principles of the welfare state have not changed drastically from the general or universal model.[35] Nevertheless, the reforms have transformed it substantially and the Swedish model as it appeared in 1980 is probably dead. Many of the reforms share the common features of increasing competition and freedom of choice.[36] Theoretically, the changes can be said to take Sweden closer to a capitalist welfare state, after having had a period of very high government involvement in the economy.

---

[35] See for instance Bergh (2004), Rothstein and Lindbom (2004), Castles (2004), Timonen (2001) and Kautto (1999).

[36] A question mark needs to be added regarding EU membership, which is often said to promote a competitive market economy as far as the single market is concerned, but also involves a significant amount of regulations, tariffs and subsidies.

Political Consensus

An interesting aspect of the Swedish reforms is their bloc-transcending political support, either directly through a cross-bloc agreement, or indirectly by a reform being introduced by one political bloc and then being accepted by the other bloc afterwards.

The right-wing government that took over office in autumn 1991 is sometimes portrayed as a government that immediately threw itself into liberalizations and deregulations. This is not a faulty illustration, but it is worth pointing out that the flying start was made possible because much had already been prepared and processed in committees. As an example, one central document concerning deregulation of the electricity market, the postal market and domestic aviation is the proposal *1990/91:81 Om näringspolitik för tillväxt* (Trade and industry policies for economic growth), which was put on the table by the Social Democratic government. This government had also carried out the deregulation of the taxi market in 1990, which the right-wing government had to evaluate promptly and then introduce supplementary regulations regarding, for example, improved pricing information and special taxi driver licences, so that the market would function efficiently.

Another example is the division of railway traffic into commercially profitable routes, which could be purchased, and non-profitable routes that nevertheless could be justified for socio-economic reasons given the covering of costs by the government. Together with the division of the rail network into core networks and county railways, these changes set out the conditions necessary for a future, competition-exposed purchasing of the railway traffic.

Another palpable sign of political unanimity is that many other typically right-wing reforms that were introduced by the Bildt government were allowed to remain even after the Social Democratic government took over office in 1994. Among them we find, for example, the allowance systems which were used to combine tax financing with freedom of choice and competition within, primarily, school education but also in other areas covered by the public sector.

The agreement surrounding the Swedish reforms is particularly remarkable, seen against the wide-ranging literature that describes the problems involved when large welfare states need to undergo reform (Pierson, 2001). The Swedish consensus concerning reforms can, however, be better understood if placed in a historic context. This will be done in the next chapter.

5. The capitalist welfare state's bloc-transcending history

It may seem surprising that a political bloc-transcending unanimity has surrounded so many important changes in such a short time, as was shown in the previous chapter. In fact, however, the rapid pace of transformation and political agreement is very much in line with Swedish political history. As noted already by Anton (1969), cross-bloc consensus where important changes are concerned and a pragmatic stance towards political ideologies are characteristic of Sweden.

Judging by the political parties' rhetoric, it often seems as if Swedish political history has been one long, vicious battle between the Right and the Left. It is also easy to get the impression that the Social Democrats have won more or less all important discussions. Certainly, there have been intense political battles, and Sweden is to a large extent defined by social democratic thinking. However, Swedish social democracy has had a very pragmatic relationship to capitalism, and the right-wing parties have not always tried to steer Sweden down a different path as regards welfare policy. A review of the twentieth century's party political history will show that there have indeed been some classic conflicts between the Right and the Left, but they are relatively few. In practice, the capitalist welfare state has to be considered a bloc-transcending project.[1] In order to support this argument, a few historical events will be revisited, starting with the origin of the welfare state and ending with the most recent right-wing government in Sweden which came to power in 2006.

THE ORIGIN OF THE WELFARE STATE

We have already seen that many of the reforms that explain the golden years in Sweden were introduced during the 1800s. Perhaps unsurprisingly it was often Liberal politicians who pushed for market economy reforms. A good deal of literature, for example, points to the central role

[1] A similar reflection is made by Bo Södersten (1991) in the book with the telling title *Capitalism Built this Country (Kapitalismen byggde Landet)*. See also Lewin (1992).

of the Liberal Johan August Gripenstedt as, among other things, Minister of Finance 1856–66, partly for the expansion of the railways, and partly for tariff reductions and free trade in grain – see Jörnmark (2004), Schön (2000), Norberg (1999) and Ohlsson (1994).

Perhaps more surprisingly, Sweden also had Conservative or right-wing governments in the 1910s, when early social insurance was introduced. The concept of building a welfare state on a capitalist foundation is, in actual fact, just as liberal (in the European sense of the word) as it is social democratic. Therborn (1994) pinpoints something important by noting that the Swedish Socialists did not oppose social reforms just because Conservative governments initiated them. As an example, he mentions how Hjalmar Branting in 1898 chose to support the Conservative government's pensions proposal, arguing that even weak reforms could be used as a starting point for future improvements. The 1913 pension reform was based on an assessment initiated earlier in 1884, dominated by progressive liberals who favoured social reforms. The appointed working group wanted the insurance to include 'workers and equals' – essentially the entire population.[2] Supported by Branting's own speeches and writings, Esping-Andersen (1994) concludes that the need to win political support from the workers was an important explanation as to why the Social Democrats accepted the general welfare model.

PROPERTY RIGHTS AND INHERITANCE TAX

Shortly after the introduction of social insurance, there was significant political disagreement relating to property rights and inheritance in 1928. The Liberal government then in office, together with the Social Democrats, pushed through a restriction on the right of inheritance beyond cousins. The Social Democrats wanted to push legislation even further, while the Right argued that the new entitlement to inheritance was only trumped by Soviet Russia in radicalism.[3]

To illustrate the Social Democrats' socialist view on this issue, a particular motion in the first chamber, signed by Gustav Möller, Richard Sandler and Ernst Wigforss is often cited. The proposal involved drastic changes to inheritance tax in order to reduce private wealth. The argument was that 'poverty is tolerated by equanimity when shared among all.

---

[2] A common interpretation is that the Swedish municipalities were so numerous and so small that the spreading of risks was not viable: the pressure on the municipalities' poverty relief would be implausibly high without a national pensions system.

[3] Källström (1991).

It becomes unbearable when it day after day can be compared to others' excess.'[4] Arguments of this kind gave the so-called Cossack-election in 1928 a sharp ideological twist.

With the benefit of hindsight, a certain amount of pragmatism is discernible even on this issue: Källström (1991) shows that Möller, Sandler and Wigforss described their objective as one that 'in the best way possible promotes the equalization of wealth without seriously becoming an impediment to personal savings' (my translation, p. 4). The Social Democrats did not oppose the idea of private property rights, even though they preferred a more restricted domain. There is probably much truth in the political scientist Leif Lewin's interpretation of the Social Democrats' pragmatic approach towards private ownership: why slaughter the goose that lays golden eggs?[5]

CONTINUED SOCIAL REFORMS AND SOCIAL DEMOCRATIC HEGEMONY

Sweden's remarkably stable period of Social Democratic rule began when Per Albin Hansson won the election in 1932. The social reforms continued, albeit possibly with a slightly different nature: a Compulsory Holidays Act which gave workers the right to two weeks of holiday was introduced, and a maternity benefit was introduced to provide support to new mothers. A longer holiday period has since been a recurring demand from the Social Democrats.

From 1936 until 1976 the Social Democrats were constantly in government, either alone, in coalition with the Farmers Alliance (now the Centre Party), or in the coalition government during the Second World War. Therborn (1994) shows that the Social Democratic Party's exclusive position in Sweden is unique among the world's parliamentary democracies. The party's dominance in Sweden exceeds that in Denmark, Norway, Australia and Austria. It also surpasses that of Japan's Liberal Democrats and Canada's Liberal Party.

It bears emphasizing that the right-wing opposition was not without influence during this period. When the Social Democrats after the Second World War presented far-reaching socialization plans, the Liberal Party, under the leadership of the economist Bertil Ohlin, gained many votes in the 1948 election. Further, the employers' side, in the form of the Swedish Industrial Fund, were very active participants in the debate on economic planning which raged during these years. The Social Democrats retained

---

[4] Quoted from Ernst Wigforss' memoirs by Källström (1991, p. 3, my translation).
[5] Quoted by Källström (1991, p. 9).

power and the social reforms continued – but the Liberal Party's electoral success is often argued to have contributed to the Social Democratic Party becoming more prudent in terms of their far-reaching socialization plans. Moreover, reality had proven that economic planning measures were superfluous when it came to firing up the economy after the Second World War. The pragmatic Swedish Social Democrats thus continued to build the welfare state on a capitalist foundation.

In the newspaper *Dagens Nyheter* in 1956, the political scientist Jörgen Westerståhl coined the term 'service democracy', describing how ideologically convinced politicians in Sweden had been replaced by a new type of politician who, irrespective of their ideological base, would compete to solve the problems of different groups in society. A telling quote from the *Dagens Nyheter* article reads as follows: 'at times, one has the impression that the proposed remedies exist even before those affected have become aware of the problems themselves.'[6]

THE PENSION DISPUTE IN THE 1950s – CONSENSUS IN THE 1990s

In the 1950s, one of the most important political conflicts in the building of the Swedish welfare state was the conflict regarding the design of the pension system. Pension systems can be divided into the pay-as-you-go type (PAYG) and the funded type. In the first, the working generations pay the pensions for those who are retired. In the latter, pensions are based on individual savings. The Social Democratic Party's proposal on income-related pensions – line 1 in the referendum held in 1957 – was based on a compulsory, income-related pay-as-you-go system with only limited correlation between the fees that were paid in and the pension that was paid out. The Right and the Liberal Party also advocated a compulsory system, but preferred a funded solution and a strong connection between fees and benefits (line 2). A third alternative prescribed a voluntary system and was supported only by the Centre Party.

The referendum resulted in a somewhat ambiguous outcome (as they often do with three or more alternatives). Line 1 received 45.8 per cent of votes, line 2 received 15 per cent and line 3 received 35.3 per cent of votes. The Social Democrats' proposal was accepted by parliament in 1959, with a margin of one vote after the Liberal Member of Parliament Ture Königson abstained from voting, thereby ensuring majority for the Social Democratic alternative.

[6] Quote from Nilsson (2004).

Hence, there was agreement across the political blocs on a compulsory, income-related pensions system. The outcome of the Social Democratic parliamentary victory was that pensions savings ended up in the national pensions funds (the so-called AP-fonderna), which enabled the government to manage savings and investments.

The pension system introduced in 1960 turned out to be rather short-lived, being phased out in the 1990s. The spirit of consensus is clearly manifest in the new system, which is supported by both the Social Democrats and the right-wing parties. Because the new system combines a pay-as-you-go part with an individually funded part, it can be described as a compromise between line 1 and line 2 of the 1950s pensions dispute.

THE RIGHT-WING GOVERNMENT 1976–82

The most obvious indication that the right-wing parties had not spent all their many years in opposition drawing up an alternative society with a completely different type of welfare state, came in 1976 when they came to power for the first time in 40 years. The new government undoubtedly wanted to show the voters that the Social Democrats were not the only ones who could push through social reforms. If anything, what changed was the acceleration of the passing of reforms increasing public expenditure.[7]

The unfortunate macroeconomic policies of the 1970s also held support in both political blocs. After the first right-wing government had collapsed due to disagreement over the introduction of nuclear power in Sweden (opposed by the Centre Party), a Liberal minority government held office in 1978–79. Together with the Social Democrats, the Liberals introduced an employment guarantee for Swedish shipyard workers. For the fiscal year of 1978–79, the subsidies per employee in the shipyard and textile and clothing industry were more than double the average wage costs of the employer. Myhrman (1994) points out that the Öresund shipyard in Landskrona continued to run despite bringing in less than 50 per cent of costs. Losses would have been cut if the components had been sold on directly instead of being assembled into a ship.

The progressiveness of the tax rate schedule continued to increase under the right-wing government, but in 1981 the Centre Party and the Liberal Party came to an agreement with the Social Democrats to reduce marginal taxes with the so-called 'wonderful night of tax reform'. The agreement was partly broken by the Social Democrats later on in the 1980s, but towards the end of the decade it was time for yet another significant,

[7] Garme (2001).

bloc-transcending tax reform, this time between the Liberal Party and the Social Democratic Party.

Hence, the tendency was not for socialist governments to increase tax progressiveness, while conservative governments lowered it. In fact, during the 1970s there was agreement between the blocs to make taxation more progressive, and in the 1980s to make it less so.

EMPLOYEE FUNDS

The solidaric wage policies resulted in large profits in successful firms. Within the Swedish Trade Union Confederation (LO), this was interpreted as a reason to introduce employee power over at least part of the profits. In 1976 the LO congress backed a fund proposal that had been put forward by Rudolf Meidner, Gunnar Fond and Anna Hedborg, which forced the Social Democrats to take action.[8] The proposal suggested directing 20 per cent of corporate profits into funds controlled by employees via the trade unions. The Social Democratic reaction was not very enthusiastic and many party members were probably surprised to learn how far LO wanted to go in this issue.

When the Social Democrats returned to power in 1982, Kjell-Olof Feldt became Minister of Finance. Feldt had assessed the issue of employee funds, and the proposal, which was passed in 1983, outlined five funds that at a maximum were allowed to own 8 per cent of a company's shares. The funds would be used for providing venture capital, and it was made clear to LO that this would be the entire extent of the reform, and not a first step towards economic democracy (or socialism, which was the term preferred by those opposed to the funds). The introduction of employee funds triggered substantial opposition, and on 4 October 1983 more than 20 000 people demonstrated in Stockholm. In 1992, the newly elected Bildt government abolished the funds and the money eventually went into the pensions system and a number of research foundations.

LEX PYSSLINGEN – THE CONTROVERSY ON CHILD CARE FOR PROFIT

In 1984 the Social Democratic Minister of Finance, Kjell-Olof Feldt, mentioned in an interview, also published as a book (Ahlqvist and Engqvist, 1984), that in terms of child care, he was not opposed to freedom of

[8] Meidner et al. (1975).

choice between different types of tax-financed alternatives.[9] Nevertheless, that same year, the Social Democrats introduced a law which prohibited government subsidizing of private day-care in the form of limited companies.[10] Over the next few years, parental cooperatives became accepted as an alternative in the childcare sector. During the late 1980s, the issue of freedom of choice and welfare service provision run for profit divided the Social Democrats – and it still does so today. Over time, however, Feldt's standpoint has become less controversial, and privately run elderly care and childcare are common also in municipalities governed by the Social Democrats. But the debate on welfare service provision for profit would become heated again in the 2010s, as described below.

A NEW RIGHT-WING GOVERNMENT 1991–94

The right-wing minority government elected in 1991 and in office until 1994 behaved differently from the governments that held office from 1976 until 1982. There was now a clear market economy reform agenda, presented by the moderates and the liberals before the 1991 election in the New Start for Sweden (*Ny start för Sverige*) programme. Albeit with a difference in emphasis, both the Social Democrats and the right-wing parties are usually keen to stress that what were pursued during the Bildt government were right-wing policies.

Nevertheless, there are many signs of consensus during this period as well. First of all, the new government could move rapidly with several reforms – because they had already been initiated or prepared by the Social Democrats. As already mentioned, several of the deregulations associated with the right-wing government had been through committee assessment and initiated while the Social Democrats were in power. The credit and currency deregulation took place during Social Democratic government, as did the taxation reform and the submission of the application for Swedish EC membership. Even the pensions reform was backed by both the Social Democrats and the right-wing parties, and consequently the old dispute regarding the ATP system could be put aside. For many changes, the Social Democratic reluctance was a question of wanting to proceed with the deregulations at a slower pace.

In other areas, the Social Democrats protested strongly against many

---

[9] Feldt (1984).

[10] The so-called '*Lex Pysslingen*', which roughly translates as the 'Tiny Tots Act', after the then newly formed *Pysslingen Förskolor och Skolor AB* (Tiny Tots Pre-schools and Schools Ltd).

of the right-wing government's decisions, but still maintained most of the reforms when they came back to power. For example, there were harsh protests when the Bildt government lowered the unemployment benefit from 90 to 80 per cent, but the next Social Democratic government led by Göran Persson decided to decrease it further to 75 per cent, eventually increasing it to 80 per cent again.

Perhaps the best illustration that the consensus thinking still prevailed during this period, was during the turbulence on the European currency markets which put the fixed exchange rate for the Swedish Krona under a lot of pressure. In this situation, the right-wing government chose to seek support from the Social Democrats, who responded by accepting austerity measures in order to save the Swedish economy's and currency's long-term credibility.

With the benefit of hindsight, it is clear that these measures came far too late and that the defence of the Krona most likely was doomed to fail from the start. But when the Krona depreciated on 19 November 1992, it was a failure not only for the Bildt government, but for the entire political establishment, including the Social Democrats, who at that point had decided that Sweden should try to weather the crisis of the 1990s without opting for the, in the short-term, easiest way out which was to let the exchange rate fall.

The most obvious example of actual political conflict, rather than de facto consensus on reforms, concerns labour-market legislation. The Social Democratic government had put forward a number of changes by setting up a committee to discuss restrictions on the trade unions' negotiation and industrial action rights.[11] But the changes that the right-wing government introduced – the ability to make two exceptions to the last hired, first fired rule, as well as a compulsory unemployment insurance that was not under trade union administration – were immediately abolished by the Social Democrats after the change of government in 1994.

2006 AND ONWARDS: NEW MODERATES, LOWER TAXES AND DEBATE ON WELFARE SERVICE PROVISION FOR PROFIT

After Social Democratic victories in the 1994, 1998 and 2002 elections, the moderates re-evaluated their proposals and strategies, and in 2003 Fredrik Reinfeldt replaced Bo Lundgren as party leader. The party started calling themselves the New Moderates (*Nya moderaterna*) and even used the label

---

[11] SOU (1991:13), The rules on the labour market (*Spelreglerna på arbetsmarknaden*).

'Sweden's new labour party'. The rhetoric became more friendly towards labour unions, the welfare state and the Swedish model in general, and promises of future tax cuts were redirected from lowering the top marginal income taxes to the introduction of an earned income tax credit.[12]

After taking a clear step towards the centre, the moderates were very successful in the 2006 election, and Sweden was run by a right-wing majority government for four years. As it turns out, the New Moderates lowered total tax revenue much more than the Bildt government in the early 1990s. Moreover, the government was re-elected in 2010. Despite a good election result, where the moderates increased their vote share from 26 to 30 per cent, the government lost its majority in parliament when the Sweden Democrats (*Sverigedemokraterna*) entered parliament for the first time. Most importantly, the de facto consensus holds: the Social Democrats protested against each step in the earned income tax credit, but also stated that they would not revoke the reforms when they returned to power.

While the Reinfeldt governments 2006–14 did not annoy the union movement by introducing mandatory unemployment insurance or by changing the employment protection laws (as the Bildt government in 1991–94 did), changes in other areas have been far-reaching. When it comes to the generosity of unemployment insurance and sickness benefit, there has been more political controversy, but it remains to be seen what big changes will be made when the Social Democrats return to office.

Lindbom notes that regarding social insurance policies, the New Moderates are in many ways more radical than the old moderates were in the 1980s. As an explanation, he suggests that new possibilities to propose cutbacks presented themselves as the Social Democrats implemented cutbacks. One example is the debate regarding stricter rules for sickness benefit, introduced by the right-wing government to increase labour force participation. These rules were not popular, and received criticism from the opposition. But as shown by Johnson (2010), the right-wing parties and the Social Democrats share a similar analysis of the problems, and Johnson criticizes changes made to the possibilities for rehabilitation previously implemented by the Social Democrats in the 1990s.

During this period, the debate on for-profit provision of tax financed welfare services intensified for many reasons. The right-wing government implemented a law according to which all counties must allow freedom of choice in primary care. Another reason was that the Swedish school system seemed to deteriorate, and according to some, independent schools

---

[12] See Lindbom (2008) for an analysis of the new moderates. Lindbom argues that the new party leadership came to the conclusion that many voters doubted that large tax cuts were compatible with sound public finances.

run for profit were to blame. To what extent this debate changes the degree of consensus in Swedish politics remains to be seen. For a long time, the issue of for-profit provision of welfare services has been highly controversial within the Social Democrats, where those with a more state-centred view tend to be more sceptical (Lindbom, 2013).

CONCLUSION: THE CAPITALIST WELFARE STATE ENJOYS SUPPORT ACROSS THE POLITICAL BLOCS

It is clear that many of the significant reforms that were carried out saw agreement across the political blocs. When battles *have* been fought between the Right and the Left, it is not the case that the Left systematically won, which is shown in the summary in Table 5.1.

A similar conclusion is reached by Uddhammar (1993) by analysing party-political dividing lines during the twentieth century. He finds considerable agreement in seven out of eight key decisions on pensions during the 1900s (the exception is the ATP decision after the 1957 referendum described above). Uddhammar also finds a considerable amount of agreement regarding support to families with children and close to absolute unanimity regarding both the extent of, and the principle of distribution for, government subsidies for public child care.[13]

The conclusion is that both political blocs can take pride in Sweden's achievements during the golden years, and both blocs bear responsibility for the problems that became evident in the 1970s. Most importantly, both blocs contributed to the substantial increase in economic freedom that took place in Sweden during the last two decades of the twentieth century.

Understanding the Consensus on Swedish Welfare State Reforms

In 1980, Sweden was a highly regulated economy with several state monopolies and low levels of economic freedom. Less than twenty years later, liberal reforms had turned Sweden into one of the world's most open economies with a remarkable increase in economic freedom. Bergh and Erlingsson (2009) seek to understand how the Swedish style of policy

---

[13] Uddhammar nevertheless also points to a certain amount of disagreement regarding the public tax levelling between Swedish municipalities. However, the disagreement does not follow the classic Left–Right dimension, since the Centre Party from time to time has wanted more redistribution between the municipalities than the Social Democrats. This suggests that the conflict between city and countryside has been at least as important in Swedish politics as the Left–Right divide.

Table 5.1   *Five important battles between the Right and the Left during the twentieth century*

Dispute	Content	Current situation
The 1928 conflict regarding property rights and inheritance taxation	Out of three alternatives – the Conservative, the Liberal and the Social Democratic – the Liberals won. The inheritance tax was restricted, but less than the Social Democrats had demanded.	The inheritance tax was abolished on 1 January 2005.
The debate on economic planning, 1944–48.	The labour movement's post-war programme in 1944 drew up far-reaching industrial policy interventions with the aim of counteracting an anticipated economic recession after the end of the war.	The Social Democrats won the election in 1948, but the electoral success of the Liberals put nationalization plans on the back-burner.
The ATP conflict in 1957 concerning compulsory pensions savings.	Three lines. voluntary (Cen), compulsory, funded system (Cons, Lib), compulsory, distributive system (SD). The line taken by the Social Democrats won by one vote in parliament.	A new system was introduced in the 1990s. The new system has clear elements of what the Conservatives and Liberals pushed for in the ATP dispute.
The employee funds conflict, starting 1975.	Parliament decides to introduce employee funds in 1983. The funds are nevertheless considerably less far-reaching than the proposal LO pushed in 1976.	The employee funds were phased out in 1992.
The notion of choice and profit within the welfare sector, the 1980s and forward.	The so-called Tiny Tots Act (*Lex Pysslingen*) prohibited the allocation of government subsidies to private day-care in the form of limited companies. Alternative management forms slowly appeared and the Tiny Tots Act was abolished in 1992.	An increase of privately run services within most sectors. Intense debate on for-profit providers of tax financed welfare services after 2010.

making produced this surprising outcome by highlighting three complementary factors:

1. Policy making in Sweden has always been influenced by, and intimately connected to, social science.
2. Government commissions have functioned as 'early warning systems', pointing out future challenges and creating a common way to perceive problems.
3. Political consensus has evolved as a feature of the Swedish style of policy making. The approach to policy making has been rationalistic, technocratic and pragmatic.

An important effect of a thorough and forward-looking committee system is that the need for reforms can be identified with a good amount of foresight. As a result there is more time to find political compromises. For example, Marier (2005) notes the important role played by bureaucrats and committees in the Swedish pensions reform, and Selen and Stahlberg (2007) point to the importance of the phasing-in time for ensuring political support for the reform. Anton (1969) was one of the first to underscore the important role of the committees in explaining Swedish political consensus, and according to Bergh and Erlingsson (2009), this explanatory model is also applicable to the reform period of the 1980s and 1990s.

6. The consequences of increasing competition

Is it possible to evaluate the consequences of the reforms towards increasing competition described in the previous chapter? In some cases the answer is yes – but a large number of caveats apply. This chapter describes how some reforms could theoretically be expected to work, discusses how evaluation can be made and summarizes empirical research on the consequences of deregulations, competitive procurement, voucher systems and capitation reforms in health care.

THEORETICAL CONSIDERATIONS: WHEN DOES COMPETITION INCREASE EFFICIENCY?

Potentially, there are three reasons for increasing the level of competition in the provision of welfare services. First, competition between producers can lead to lower costs and higher quality. Second, consumer preferences can be better satisfied if offered the choice between different types of producers. Third, competition creates incentives for innovation and the development of new products and services via the profit motive.

These effects do not appear automatically whenever a reform leads to more competition. It has to be easy for consumers to attain the correct information about the product or service in question. There have to be several alternatives on the market to choose between. Changing from one alternative to another should not be associated with high costs.[1]

Shleifer (1998) lists a number of situations when public production may be preferable to private:

- when there is a significant possibility of saving money by lowering quality which cannot be safe-guarded against by the design of the contract;

---

[1] Importantly, it is sufficient that some consumers choose actively for competition to have the desired effects. Theoretically the effect comes from giving citizens the option to chose, rather than from choice per se.

- when it is not important to create incentives for innovation;
- when there is weak competition on the private market, which in practice works to limit consumer choice;
- when it is difficult for consumers to assess different actors' quality through reputation mechanisms.

As is apparent, the guidance offered is not crystal clear: within health care it is often difficult for patients to assess the quality of the provided care – but at the same time strong incentives for innovation are vital.

It should be stressed that incentives for innovation are not necessarily non-existent in public output. However, if the profit motive is at least one of the drivers behind innovations which enable more efficient use of resources, the ambition to keep the profit motive away from the health sector will in the long run lead to a lower rate of innovation.

Shleifer's first point regarding contract design is crucial for private providers in the publicly financed welfare services. The reason is that the reforms can be viewed as partial privatization, where financing and regulation remain a public responsibility, and the public sector must sign a contract with the private provider on the provision.

As shown by Table 6.1, most reforms have followed the continuous arrow, that is introducing private provision while maintaining public financing and regulation. This is important because competition can be expected to lead to innovation, lower prices and higher quality only when financing is also private. This allows providers to compete both by lowering prices and by increasing quality. For example, on a well-functioning market there will be low-quality, low-price health care or schooling for those with low ability to pay, and better and more expensive products targeted towards the high-income earners.[2]

In many cases, financing is kept public because the distributive outcomes of full privatization are not desirable. In practice, this means that policy makers cannot rely on competition to improve both quality and lower costs. Instead, they have a choice between two options. One option is to fix the cost and use competition among providers to improve quality. Another option is to fix the quality and use competition among providers to lower the costs. For both options to work as intended, the contract between the public sector and the private provider is crucial. While costs and some aspects of quality are easy to measure and put in a contract,

---

[2] Note that low price and low quality does not necessarily mean low value for money. Consider for example the market for fast food or cars, where both provision and financing is private. There are good value-for-money alternatives both in the high-end and the low-end of these markets – but the absolute quality level will vary because people's willingness to pay varies.

Table 6.1   Complete versus partial privatization

		Financing and regulation	
		Public	Private
Provision	Public		
	Private		

other aspects of quality are hard to measure and in some cases even hard to observe.

For example, one might want the waiting time for a place in a care home for the elderly to be a maximum of three months, while the residents also should be treated with dignity and respect. The first objective is easily quantified and expressed in a contract, while the second is more problematic. If only the first objective is written into the contract, there is a risk that the objective concerning dignity is neglected.[3]

METHODOLOGICAL CONSIDERATIONS: CAN WE MEASURE THE EFFECTS OF COMPETITION?

When political reforms are evaluated, it is easy to fall into the so-called *post hoc* trap. The *post hoc* trap is when events which follow a certain change automatically are assumed to be caused by the change. This is not necessarily the case.[4]

After the most intensive periods of change, Sweden has for example experienced increased economic growth, higher rates of unemployment, and more achievements in athletics. However, there is not necessarily a causal connection in any of the cases. Simply observing certain variables of interest before and after a reform towards more competition is not

---

[3] In Hart et al. (1997) American prisons are mentioned as an example of where private management in some cases has led to a reduction in costs but also to an increase in violence towards the prisoners (which is more difficult to formulate in a contract).

[4] 'Post hoc, ergo propter hoc' is Latin for 'after this, thus because of this' and is one of the most common logical fallacies. The fact that a cold may pass after one has scoffed a considerable amount of ginger, does not, as many know, mean that the ginger caused the recovery.

enough to evaluate the reform. If you observe an improvement, this might have happened anyway. If you observe a decline, things might have been even worse without the reform. Thus, as a minimum, one should also be able to present a theoretical link on the mechanism through which competition affects the outcome studied, and it should preferably be possible to find empirical evidence of these mechanisms actually occurring.

Another potential pitfall when it comes to evaluation of competition from private providers in the provision of welfare services is to compare private providers with public sector providers. If competition has any effects, it is likely to affect both public and private providers. As a result, finding that private and public providers are similar is not necessarily a sign that competition is not working (and finding differences is not necessarily a sign that it is).

The situation is similar to the discussion in Box 2.1 (page 7) on the causal effects of institutions such as property rights. For evaluation purposes, the ideal set-up would be for example if some, randomly chosen, municipalities introduced a voucher system or competitive procurement, and that other municipalities did not. In the absence of such controlled experiments, researchers can instead compare municipalities with many private providers to municipalities with few private providers, and try to control for other differences between municipalities that might affect the outcome studied. Sometimes it is also possible to compare changes over time, by for example studying how test results have changed in municipalities where the number of independent schools have changed.

EMPIRICAL RESULTS

Deregulations

The Swedish Agency for Public Management (Statskontoret), has assessed six of the Swedish deregulations initiated during the 1990s. The situation post-deregulation is summarized in Table 6.2. The points indicate the occurrence of competition-restricting circumstances and problems relating to market establishment. Points in brackets indicate less severe problems. The table suggests that full competition does not exist in any of the six markets even after deregulation.

The outcome of the electricity market deregulation is widely debated because the price of electricity has gone up since the deregulation. But many different factors contribute to a higher electricity price, many of which are political decisions taken for environmental reasons: closing the Barsebäck nuclear power plant and increasing taxes on energy. The central issue

Table 6.2   *Restrictions on competition on six deregulated markets*

	Formal monopolies	Remaining barriers to establishment	Occurrence of buyer monopolies	Competition-biased access to infrastructure	Company concentration and problem of dominance	Weak incentives for consumers to act
Electricity	⊙	⊙				•
Postal service		⊙			•	
Telecoms		⊙		•	•	•
Domestic aviation	•	•	⊙	⊙	•	
Railways	•	•	⊙	⊙	•	⊙
Taxi			⊙		⊙	•

Source: Statskontoret (2004, p. 9).

concerns how electricity prices are set by an international market, where EU carbon dioxide emissions trading has further increased prices: significant parts of Europe's energy does, after all, come from coal and oil. According to Statskontoret, the deregulation of the Swedish electricity market has nevertheless led to a more rational use of resources and a reduction in overcapacity. Competition is limited though, as state-owned Vattenfall is responsible for almost half of the production. Another problem is that consumers only have weak incentives to change their electricity provider. More recently, Brännlund et al. (2012) conclude that the Nordic market for electricity works as expected, with price changes driven by changes in supply and demand.

On the postal market, Statskontoret has noted that the conversion of the state-owned Posten AB into a company seems to have led to higher efficiency. The prices better reflect the different products' actual costs, new methods of production have been introduced and a certain amount of product development has taken place. Competition is, however, still weak with the exception of certain segments of the market.

The deregulated telecommunications market is often paraded as a successful example of deregulation. Competition has increased and prices have come down, even though mobile phone rates for a long while were higher than in other countries. Product development has been very strong. An important factor for making competition work was the expansion in 2003 of the law on phone number portability to include mobile phone numbers, thereby substantially lowering the transaction costs for consumers switching providers.

The domestic aviation market has not developed as successfully. For a long period of time, there were considerable price differences between expensive domestic flights and cheap international flights, as low-cost airlines put pressure on prices. Competition is limited with the partly international SAS as the main actor. More recently, however, new, smaller actors have established themselves on the market and prices have fallen.

The railway market is plagued by similar problems. Competition is scarce due to the state monopoly on profitable passenger transport and control of the freight market. The price of passenger transport increased more than the general price level. The Swedish state railway companies (SJ AB and Green Cargo AB) continue to operate at a loss despite having set commercial goals and repeatedly receiving infusions of capital from the state. Recently, a number of reforms have increased competition further, but these reforms have not yet been evaluated.[5]

The deregulation of the taxi market has, according to Statskontoret,

---

[5] For example, since 2009, Veolia transport has offered a train service between Malmö and Stockholm, directly competing with the former monopolist SJ.

resulted in an increase in competition, especially in larger cities, as well as an increase in the supply of taxis. Customer service has also improved as waiting times have become shorter. In an international literature study, Moore and Balaker (2006) point out that of a total of 28 studies on taxi deregulation, 19 were positive towards the outcomes of deregulation. The negative studies were primarily completely theory-based, while all of the empirical studies came out as positive. The authors, however, argue that future research should focus more on the developments of the unlicensed taxi market.

Competitive Procurement

In the mid-1990s, a commission in Australia went through 203 studies of competitive procurement (Industry Commission, 1996). In almost half of the studies, savings were in the range of 10–30 per cent. The remaining studies were equally divided between those with bigger savings and those with smaller savings. Arthursson and Ekelund (2004) find similar results in a more recent literature review. The possibility of increasing effectiveness lies at around 30 per cent for transportation and technical businesses and at 10 per cent for health care and general care.

These studies have, however, been criticized. Andersson (2002) identifies two main arguments in the criticism. First, the costs of administration and follow-up can become considerable. Secondly, cost savings may partly come from lowering wages, and in that case it is not so much a socio-economic efficiency profit as redistribution from public employees to taxpayers. According to Domberger and Jensen (1997) experience nevertheless shows that cost savings primarily can be explained by better management, more flexible work methods, more efficient use of capital and a higher pace of innovation – not by wage reductions.

Figures on cost savings must also be looked at in relation to the quality of the services carried out. However, for the same reason that quality can be difficult to write into a contract, it is also difficult to measure. Some of the studies that have attempted this are referred to in Domberger and Rimmer (1994), but there is no consensus regarding the effect on quality. Further, from the literature it has also become evident that private contractors are often not more effective than public: rather, it is competition in itself that creates good incentives for both private and public producers – see Domberger et al. (1995).

To summarize the state of research, it seems safe to say that competitive procurement can generate substantial savings when introduced for the first time. The long-run effects are harder to analyse. Furthermore, the contracts between public sectors and private providers must be carefully drawn up so that savings are not made at the expense of quality.

Elderly Care and Health care

Meagher and Szebehely (2013) summarize research on competitive procurement (what they call marketization) of residential care. For Sweden, they report some evidence of saving in first-generation contracts, most likely related to the fact that units run for profit have lower staffing levels, lower training levels and more hourly employment. However, for-profit units also have higher process quality and there seems to be no difference in user satisfaction. The pattern that competitive procurement reduces costs without lowering subjectively perceived quality is confirmed by Bergman et al. (2012), who also find a positive effect on survival rate.[6] For home care services, Meagher and Szebehely (2013) report no evidence of saving and some evidence of increased transaction costs. International studies have found less encouraging results. For example, Chou (2002) finds that for-profit homes provide lower quality than non-profit rivals when the client has no close living relatives or is suffering from dementia, but not otherwise.

When it comes to the use of Diagnosis Related Groups (DRG) and the Prospective Payment System (PPS) in health care, several international evaluations exist, as these systems have been used a great deal since their introduction in the USA in the early 1980s. Hamada et al. (2012) summarize the literature by noting that findings demonstrate that DRG/PPS reduce cost and average length of stay without affecting health care quality. A Swedish study by Gerdtham et al. (1999) points to potential savings of about 13 per cent from switching from budget-based allocation to an output-based allocation.

Regarding the law on freedom of choice, a report by the Swedish Competition Authority (Konkurrensverket, 2012) finds an increasing supply of primary health centres (*vårdcentraler*) and also notes that the quality perceived by patients is higher in areas with more competition, in both publicly and privately run units.

Work Satisfaction

From a theoretical perspective, competition between different service providers should also have positive effects for those employed by the businesses. When there is one possible employer for many professions – namely the public sector – this should have a negative effect on wages and

---

[6] An older study with similar conclusions is Suzuki (2001), who find that the cost of elderly care is lower in municipalities with private providers, both because these are less expensive, and because competition pushes down costs of publicly run units.

working conditions. There are survey studies that suggest that workers employed by private contractors are slightly more content with their salary and ability to influence their own working situation (Svenskt Näringsliv, 2002; Kommunförbundet, 1999), but such studies are not conclusive. For example, workers who want to leave the public sector to work for private alternatives might be more satisfied because they are allowed to do so, and not because privately run units are better managed. Furthermore, it is likely that competition also in this aspect affects conditions in both private and public providers.

School Vouchers and other School Reforms

Quite a large amount of research has been carried out on the effects of school vouchers, both in Sweden and in other countries. By choosing the voucher system, costs per student are fixed and schools compete in the quality dimension by attracting students. A potential problem arises if quality as perceived by the students is different from political decision makers' perception of quality. This point is emphasized by Vlachos (2012). For example, students or parents might prefer schools where teachers are generous in their grading standards – despite evidence that stricter grading standards produce better learning outcomes (Figlio and Lucas, 2004). It may also be the case that students perceive schools to be attractive as a result of their socio-economic student composition rather than teaching quality (Rothstein, 2006).

Despite these concerns, early studies of the Swedish voucher system found the expected positive effects of competition. Bergström and Sandström (2005) found no evidence that total school expenditures increased as a result of the reform, and also found that competition from independent schools had measurable positive effects on public schools: better results achieved for a national standardized test in mathematics, higher grades and less likelihood of students leaving school without a certificate. The results were controversial, which led to a number of robustness tests being carried out by the authors and others.

A possible objection is that competition creates grade inflation and that the effect on knowledge therefore was overestimated. The authors responded that the result also appears when using national standardized tests in mathematics, which are much harder for schools to manipulate.

If independent schools are more common in certain municipalities where schools are better for other reasons that are unrelated to school competition, the result may be a result of self-selection. But the result survives including a large number of control variables. Also, a different study by Ahlin (2003) used a difference-in-difference approach and found very similar results: an increase in the proportion of pupils in independent schools by 10 per cent improves results in mathematics by 0.19 standard deviations in Bergström and Sandström's study, and by 0.17 standard deviations in Ahlin's. Similarly, Björklund et al. (2003) re-analysed the data and confirmed the results controlling for unobserved differences between municipalities that might skew the results. These results, however, indicate that weak pupils gain significantly less than strong pupils from increased competition. More recently, Böhlmark and Lindahl (2012) have confirmed the results, not only for English and maths test results but also for long-run outcomes such as propensity to enter higher education. Finally, Böhlmark et al. (2012) find that school management matters and that individual principals have a substantive impact on student outcomes. Moreover, the scope for principal discretion is larger in small schools, in voucher schools and in areas with more school competition.

On the other hand, Vlachos (2010) finds evidence of competition leading to grade inflation. It is also the case that the segregation, as measured by between-school variation of grades, has increased (Nordström Skans and Åslund, 2010).[7] Regarding the latter, Lindbom (2010) argues that the main driving force behind school segregation is housing segregation, whereas Östh et al. (2013) attribute increasing segregation to structural change in the school system, including liberalized school choice. Böhlmark and Holmlund (2011) find a seemingly contradictory result in that the importance of family background for school choice has increased, but the importance of family back ground for student performance has not. A possible explanation is that peer group effects are relatively unimportant, or that high status schools have higher grades but are not necessarily better in other aspects, perhaps as a result of most municipalities complementing the school voucher with a fund meant to compensate for socio-economic disadvantages.

For some time after the introduction, voucher schools were not a very controversial political issue in Sweden. With mounting evidence of deteriorating student performance (both relative to other countries, and measured by absolute levels), the debate on school vouchers and schooling in general has become very heated.[8] A problem here is that the Swedish

---

[7] The variation in student performance between municipalities has however not increased (Böhlmark and Holmlund, 2011).

[8] Student performance in mathematics, science and reading is measured on 15-year-old pupils by the OECD Program for International Student Assessment (PISA), and the Trends in International Mathematics and Science Study (TIMSS) for pupils aged 9 to 14. The results for Sweden are summarized by Skolverket (2007, 2010 and 2012). Among the most noteworthy trends is the continuous deterioration of maths skills among Swedish pupils since 1995.

school system has changed in many ways, which makes it hard to identify the main causes of decreasing quality and increasing school segregation. In addition to the voucher system and allowing for-profit provision, there is the decentralization from state to municipalities in 1990 – though Ahlin and Mörk (2005) show that school spending as well as teacher density was in fact more equally distributed across municipalities following decentralization, and also that local tax capacity does not influence schooling resources more in the decentralized regime than in the centralized regime.

Another possible explanation is teaching methods and/or teacher quality. Grönqvist and Vlachos (2008) document a substantial decline in entering teachers' cognitive and non-cognitive abilities, but finds only negligible effects of teacher quality on student achievement.

Regarding the introduction of a new grading system in 1998, Gustafsson and Yang-Hansen (2009) show that socio-economic inequality in grades has increased more sharply after the introduction of new, goal oriented grades in 1998 – but this observation is of course only indicative.

CONCLUSIONS

All reforms have not been assessed, and the long-run effects of increasing competition are very hard to measure. From the experience so far, it seems pretty clear that competitive procurement can lead to lower costs, but contracts must be carefully designed to avoid savings at the expense of quality, and one must be careful that the savings from procurement are not thwarted by the transaction costs of the procurement procedure.

When it comes to the effect of school choice, research is still very much in progress. Tentatively, it seems to have lead to positive effects on student test scores, but also perhaps to grade inflation and probably to increased segregation between schools. It is worth noting that in 2003, Björklund et al. (2003) noted that after decentralization and the introduction of competition through the voucher system, it is crucial that outcomes are monitored closely and centrally, by for example using central grading of national tests, thereby limiting the possibilities for schools to compete by lowering standards.

It must be stressed that while competition has increased on many markets and sectors, there is still a substantial degree of intervention in most markets. The explanation is of course that the policy goal is not to maximize efficiency and innovation but also to promote an equitable distribution of, for example, health care and access to pharmaceuticals. In many cases it is more correct to speak of re-regulation rather than de-regulation.

Finally, while combining public financing and regulation with competition and private provision causes some problems and leads to many difficult decisions, the outcome observed must be compared to a counterfactual situation with either less or more competition increasing reforms, and these choices are likely to have political consequences. Bergh (2008) suggests that many reforms have made the welfare state more beneficial for upper middle-class voters, and that the reforms can be seen as a way to ensure that a majority of the voters continue to reform the welfare state. As far as attitudes towards the welfare state and tax financing of various welfare services are concerned, Svallfors (2011) shows that support for the welfare state has actually increased during the period of intense support. The problem, of course, is to say if this is a result of reforms or something that has happened despite the reforms.

7. The resilience of labour market regulation and rent control

Given the high paced reform process in different areas described in Chapter 4, it is worth emphasizing that there are areas where very little has happened, and where Sweden remains highly regulated compared to other countries. Two obvious examples are labour market regulations and the rent-controlled and highly regulated housing market.[1] In this chapter, the history of these regulations is described, the consequences are discussed and possible explanations for the absence of reform in these areas are discussed.

LABOUR MARKET REGULATIONS

The law concerning employment security was introduced in 1974 and ended the employer's right to freely terminate contracts. With a few exceptions, the law covers all forms of employment, both in the private and in the public sector. Many of the regulations in the Employment Protection Act (*Lagen om anställningsskydd*, LAS) can be replaced by central or local collective agreements. The Act builds on a few main principles:

1. Employment will normally be valid until further notice is given.
2. Dismissal is only permitted on grounds of fact.
3. Redundancy due to job shortages must follow the so-called priority rules, according to which the most recently employed will be the first to go (last hired, first fired).

Immediately after its introduction, the law was criticized by employers for not allowing a trial period of employment. After an assessment was carried out, a new law on employment security was introduced in 1982, which to a greater extent allowed employers to recruit for limited periods of time. The adjustment enabled trial periods of employment and a more

---

[1] A third example would be the state monopoly on selling alcohol, maintained for public health reasons.

flexible handling of temporary recruitment peaks and the subsequent increased demand for personnel. In 1984 the law was tightened so that any exemptions from the priority rules in terms of dismissals had to be approved by a central employee organization. The rules relating to redundancy also changed so that full salary was payable throughout the period of notice.

The set of regulations on the labour market was evaluated in 1991 in an official report (SOU 1991:13), and in the spring 1993 a committee proposed far-reaching amendments to the legislation. The trade unions were not keen on the report, and the right-wing government implemented a few of the suggestions. The amendments primarily concerned a broadening of the scope for time-limited employment and allowed employers to make at most two exceptions to the last hired, first fired rule. Due to the Social Democrats' return to government after the elections in 1994, these amendments turned out to very be short-lived.

A number of modifications which came into effect in 1997, including a new opportunity for time-limited employment, widened opportunity to negotiate local agreements and a time limit on temporary postings. In 2001 a small step back towards the changes of 1993 was taken when two exceptions to the last hired, first fired rule were allowed for firms with a maximum of ten employees (a change that gained majority because it was supported by the right-wing parties and the Green Party).

Thus, overall there has been a slight loosening of regulations in recent years, but Swedish employment security is still strict in comparison with other countries. Moreover, the changes towards more flexibility have almost exclusively concerned temporary contracts. This is in line with the trend in other countries: as noted by Boeri (2011) the reform strategy in most countries has been to increase labour market flexibility at the margin, through the deregulation of temporary contracts. This creates a labour market dualization, with relatively high job security for those with fixed contracts, and insecurity for those with temporary contracts.

As a quantitative indicator of the development, the OECD has developed an index of employment protection laws, shown in Table 7.1 for both regular and temporary contracts. Clearly, Sweden now has a relatively flexible labour market for temporary contracts, but not much has happened for regular contracts. Denmark distinguishes itself among the Scandinavian countries by having what, according to European standards, would be considered as flexible regulation.

Research on the effects of employment protection laws is summarized by Skedinger (2011). In line with theoretical expectations, stringent employment protection contributes to less turnover and job reallocation,

Table 7.1 How rigorous is employment protection legislation?

Regular contracts				Temporary contracts			
Country	1985	2000	2013	Country	1985	2000	2013
Portugal	5.0	4.6	3.2	France	3.1	3.6	3.6
Germany	2.6	2.7	2.9	Norway	3.1	3.0	3.0
Netherlands	3.1	2.9	2.8	Spain	3.8	3.25	2.6
Sweden	**2.8**	**2.7**	**2.6**	Belgium	4.6	2.4	2.4
France	2.6	2.3	2.4	Greece	4.8	4.8	2.25
Norway	2.3	2.3	2.3	Portugal	3.4	2.8	1.8
Denmark	2.2	2.1	2.2	Finland	1.25	1.6	1.6
Finland	2.8	2.3	2.2	Denmark	3.1	1.4	1.4
Greece	2.8	2.8	2.1	Germany	5.0	2.0	1.1
Spain	3.5	2.4	2.0	Switzerland	1.1	1.1	1.1
Belgium	1.8	1.8	1.8	Netherlands	1.4	0.9	0.9
Australia	1.2	1.4	1.7	Australia	0.9	0.9	0.9
Switzerland	1.6	1.6	1.6	**Sweden**	**4.1**	**1.4**	**0.8**
Ireland	1.4	1.4	1.4	Ireland	0.25	0.25	0.6
UK	1.0	1.2	1.0	UK	0.25	0.25	0.4
Canada	0.9	0.9	0.9	USA	0.25	0.25	0.25
USA	0.26	0.26	0.26	Canada	0.25	0.25	0.25

Notes: Index 0 to 6. Countries ranked according to strictness in 2013.

Source: Index from the OECD (variable names: EPRC_V1 and EPT_V1).

but seems not to have large effects on aggregate employment and unemployment. In line with the insider–outsider theory (Lindbeck and Snower, 1988), and observations made earlier for Sweden by Björklund (1982), labour market prospects for young people and other marginal groups seem to worsen as a consequence of increased stringency of the legislation.

The absence of any extensive liberalization of the Swedish labour market probably does not come as a surprise to many people. The attempt to change the last hired, first fired rule in 1993 did not go well with the unions, and the right-wing government elected in 2006 has chosen not to touch the issue. According to insider–outsider theory, the explanation is that those who benefit from the regulations are better organized and more influential than the marginal groups who more often have temporary contracts, such as young people and immigrants.

THE HOUSING MARKET AND RENT CONTROL

Rent control was introduced in Sweden in 1942 during the Second World War. The housing policy from this period is described in the social report on housing, written immediately after the end of WW2 (SOU 1945:63). The aim of the policy was straightforward: cramped living was to be eliminated and rents were to be controlled so that a well-equipped, one-bedroom flat would be let at 20 per cent of the average Swedish blue-collar worker's salary.

In effect, the rents practically remained frozen from 1942 until 1975, and the norm when setting rents was to have negotiations between tenant and landlord organizations, similar to the collective agreement-negotiations on the labour market. Rent was set according to the so-called utility value, which was supposed to reflect the standard of the flat, regardless of location. This price also functioned as a template for the private housing market. The housing market was also controlled in other ways, among other things through the ability to rank would-be tenants. Further, housing construction was regulated by government norms regarding building standards. The housing sector in Sweden has been subsidized through, among other things, a general interest rate allowance for accommodation, a supplementary housing allowance for pensioners, and general housing benefit (means tested against the applicant's income and cost of his/her accommodation).

The effects of the housing policies have been analysed repeatedly, and are often used as textbook examples of the causes of price controls: lengthy queues for housing in attractive areas, empty flats in 'troubled' municipalities. As noted by Glaeser and Luttmer (2003), most research on the social costs of rent control focuses on reduced supply and ignores the misallocation costs due to apartments not being rented by those who value them the most. Recently, Anderson and Soderberg (2012) calculated that eliminating rent control would generate welfare gains estimated at SEK 20 billion for inner Stockholm alone through more efficient allocation, thus excluding welfare gains from increased supply.

Furthermore, Meyerson et al. (1990) conclude that Swedish housing policy has resulted in too much being spent in total on housing compared to the actual willingness of people to pay. One way of understanding this is by posing the following question: how would the households that have received housing benefit to cover part of the rent have acted if they had been given the same amount of money to dispose of as they wished? Even if only a small number of households in that situation would have chosen slightly cheaper accommodation and put part of the allowance to other use, the directed subsidy has had a distortionary effect.[2]

Another effect concerns the profitability of the production of new houses: when rents do not cover full production costs, fewer are produced. Further, production has been diverted from the type of housing for which willingness to pay is high towards the type of housing targeted by political and bureaucratic decisions. According to Meyerson et al. (1990), owner-occupied flats and houses have been under-produced and flats and houses owned by the municipality have been over-produced. A clear illustration of the inefficiencies in the housing policies is the fact that for long periods of time there have been significantly more flats than there are households, but at the same time housing queues have been long.

A third outcome concerns the odd distributive effects the policy has given rise to: many tenants rent centrally located flats at a price which falls considerably below the market price.

Essentially, private property owners and taxpayers are left to pay for the pleasure in their capacity as owners of public housing, since the price is not allowed to increase to its market equivalent. Andersson and Söderberg (2005) find that people who, through their position as an elected representative, employer or through other contacts, have access to a flat with a rent set clearly below the market price, are exposed to temptations that may lead to nepotism and corruption.

After more than 60 years of rent control, Sweden's big cities are highly segregated, and it is highly doubtful whether the housing policy has had the redistributive effects that its supporters sometimes refer to. As noted by Andersson and Söderberg (2005), very few low-income earners reside in the very attractive rental apartments on Östermalm in Stockholm. Further, they point out that rent control has led to age segregation. Hence, the tenants in the rented flats in Stockholm's inner city are often older or middle-aged, while the younger tenants who are new to town are relegated to accommodation in the suburbs and surrounding areas, as well as expensive, newly built housing.

As a contrast to the controlled rental market, those who are able to get substantial mortgages or are in possession of sufficient private wealth can find accommodation on the market for detached houses and private housing cooperatives (so-called *bostadrätt*).

Andersson and Söderberg (2005) further argue that the rigid housing market has repercussions on the labour market, where mobility is reduced

---

[2] If it is possible to find an argument in support of the socio-economic value of housing being significantly higher than the individual deems it to be, subsidies could be justified – however, it is difficult to imagine what that argument would be.

for the simple reason that it is difficult to find housing in popular areas quickly.

On the whole, the difference between market rents and politically regulated systems is easy to grasp. Neither system can guarantee all inhabitants the right to live in a central location in the most popular urban areas. Hence, a selection mechanism is required. The market solution is to let willingness and ability to pay decide. In a politically controlled system, the most important mechanisms are housing queues and contacts. In those areas where regulated prices fall below market prices, like in popular metropolitan areas, visible revenue is reduced and replaced by sub-letting, inheritances, transfers and black market trading in accommodation contracts.

The political debate surrounding rent control today is remarkably similar to the debate that went on over 40 years ago when Bentzel et al. (1963) were among the first to highlight the effects of the regulation. If the potential gains from eliminating rent controls are so big, why has nothing happened? Interestingly, Lindbeck (2012) provides information that suggests that the gains from the reform may paradoxically be a reason why it has not been implemented. In the 1960s, the Social Democrats had far-reaching plans to end rent control in Sweden. Doing so would of course increase the value of houses in attractive areas, and the Social Democratic leader and Prime Minister at the time, Tage Erlander, got into a political fight with Liberal Party leader Bertil Ohlin, on whether these gains ought to be taxed or not. The fight ended with Erlander abandoning the plans to abolish rent control.

Another possible reason is that rent control is kept because it leads to lower socio-economic housing segregation. But as noted by Glaeser (2003), it is not obvious that allocation through ability to pay is more segregationist than allocation by landlord preferences or by political mechanisms.

A final factor that should be considered is that rent control in Sweden has not been put under pressure by the surrounding world in the same way that, for instance, the credit and currency regulation was: large firms could for the most part get around that one by means of international transactions, but globalization has not contributed to undermine rent control in the same way.

While a sudden abandoning of rent controls seems highly unlikely, it is worth noting that some changes have occurred that may in the long run take Sweden to a more market-based system.[3] First of all, even municipally owned housing companies must now act in a businesslike manner, which

---

[3] Boverket (2011).

decreases the differences between public and private housing. Secondly, from 2011, the rent levels that are allowed are no longer determined by the municipally owned housing companies only. Third, new production can now be excluded from the rent control for a period of 10 years. So far, however, these changes have only had marginal effects.

8. Challenges ahead: can the capitalist welfare state survive?

In the 1980s and the early 1990s, the debate on the welfare state was very different from the debate today. Many scholars predicted a dismal future for large welfare states. For example Snower (1993) argued that universal welfare states will come under budgetary pressure and concluded that welfare state services should be redirected from the middle class to the poor, turning universal welfare states into smaller targeted welfare states. The problems for the welfare states were often connected to a perceived threat from globalization (Martin and Schumann, 1997; Strange, 1996). Many argued that increased mobility of capital and labour will lead to skilled labour and capital leaving the welfare state, thus eroding the tax base. There was talk of a race to the bottom, such that welfare states would be forced to lower taxes and welfare benefits (Sinn, 2003). A related and often mentioned threat was population ageing, as falling birth rates and increasing longevity would increase expenditure on pensions and health care, putting pressure on welfare states to increase taxes further, with the risk of worsening the flight of skilled labour and capital, eroding the tax base even further.[1]

Many predicted a dismal future for Sweden in particular. In 1984 Swedish political scientist Elisabeth Langby argued that Swedish politicians would be unable to implement the changes necessary to avoid a collapse of the system. Langby specified that a pension reform was politically impossible, as was private provision of publicly financed services. Furthermore, increasing efficiency in the public sector and bringing down the budget deficit would be impossible (Langby, 1984, pp. 72–81). A similar description of the problem was given by economists Ingemar Ståhl and Kurt Wickman in a book titled *Suedosclerosis* (Ståhl and Wickman, 1993). In 1991, the Cato Institute published a report titled 'Sweden: From capitalist success to welfare-state sclerosis' (Stein, 1991).[2] Clearly, most

---

[1] For example, Andersen (2008) discusses prospects and challenges for the Scandinavian welfare state model, and focuses on demography, globalization and increasing demand for services and leisure.

[2] See also Borg (1992) for a critique of universal welfare state policies. In 2006, the same Anders Borg would be minister of finance in a new right-wing government, with different views on these issues.

of the critique came from the political Right, but there were also Social Democrats who sounded the alarm, calling for radical reforms to save the welfare state, for example (Feldt, 1994).

When the crisis of the early 1990s hit Sweden much harder than most countries, there was also considerable international interest. In October 1993, *The Economist* published an article on Sweden under the headline 'Worse and worse', describing increasing public debt, a budget deficit at 13 per cent of GDP and noting that the Swedish Krona had lost 30 per cent against the D-Mark in less than a year after the failure to defend the fixed exchange rate.[3]

Today, the debate is very different. Especially after the 2008 financial crisis, Sweden has once again become a success story, portrayed as a 'North star' and a 'Super model' by *The Economist*, and by *The Washington Post* as the 'Rockstar of recovery' after the 2008 financial crisis.[4] Perhaps most importantly, economic growth in Sweden is no longer lagging behind but rather outpacing the US and other European countries (as can be seen in Figure 3.1).

WHAT HAPPENED TO THE COLLAPSE OF THE WELFARE STATE?

Simply observing government size and economic performance over time in different countries is enough to raise doubts on the most pessimistic predictions regarding high-tax societies such as Sweden. Figure 8.1 illustrates one of the most inclusive measures of government size, total general government revenue (measured as a share of GDP using data from Eurostat), for the five European countries with highest and lowest total revenue in 1995, the year in which the high-tax countries Sweden, Finland and Austria joined the European Union. The five European countries with the highest revenue share in 1995 were Sweden, followed by Denmark, Finland, Norway and Austria, and the country with the lowest share in 1995 was Romania, followed by Cyprus, Lithuania, Switzerland and Malta.

The pattern shown in Figure 8.1 reveals no race to the bottom, but instead indicates weak convergence towards the mean. In fact, the trend upwards for countries with small government in 1995 is stronger than the trend downwards among countries with big government. Compared to the other high-tax countries, however, the trend downwards is steeper for Sweden.[5]

---

[3] *The Economist*, 9 October, 1993.
[4] *The Economist*, 9 June, 2011 and 2 February, 2013; *The Washington Post*, 24 June, 2011.
[5] These data from Eurostat include all government revenue, but the pattern is the same when using only total tax revenue as a share of GDP. The conclusion also remains when focusing on EU-15 countries only, in which case the bottom five in 1995 were the United

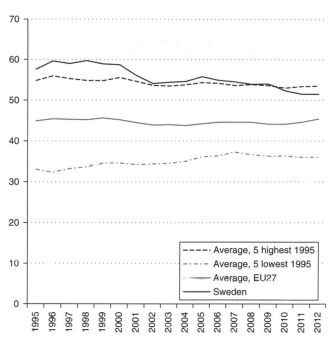

Source: Eurostat.

Figure 8.1   *Total general government revenue (% of GDP) for European countries 1995–2012*

Looking instead at growth of real GDP per capita, Table 8.1 shows that the high-tax countries have done relatively well. In fact, the countries with the highest taxes in Europe in 1995 have since then experienced above average growth (Denmark being the only exception), also outpacing many of the low-tax economies in 1995. The latter fact is even more remarkable when considering that many low-tax countries are also relatively poor and should thus be able to grow faster as a result of catching up.

Contrasting the gloomy prognoses of the 1980s and the early 1990s with the economic development that actually followed, it is relevant to ask what happened to the predicted collapse of the high-tax welfare state. Basically, there are a number of explanations, all of which have some truth to them.

First, there was some degree of exaggeration and misconception in the

Kingdom, Portugal, Spain, Ireland and Greece, and the top 5 were Sweden, Denmark, Finland, Austria and France.

Table 8.1   Annual growth of real GDP per capita, 1995–2011

Countries with biggest government sector in 1995	Annual per capita growth
Sweden	2.1%
Denmark	0.9%
Finland	2.2%
Norway	1.4%
Austria	1.7%
France	1.7%
Avg, EU-27	1.4%
Avg, EU-15	1.2%
Countries with smallest government sector in 1995 (Europe)	
Romania	2.8%
Cyprus	1.4%
Lithuania	5.7%
Switzerland	1.1%
Malta	1.1%
Countries with smallest government sector in 1995 (EU-15)	
United Kingdom	1.6%
Portugal	1.0%
Spain	0.7%
Ireland	3.2%
Greece	1.0%

Source: Own calculations based on Real Gross Domestic Product per capita from Eurostat (updated 4 October 2013).

description of the threats and challenges for the welfare state. In particular, the consequences of population ageing and increasing globalization are less problematic than previously thought.

Second, the more pessimistic welfare state predictions probably underestimated the ability of policy makers to adapt the welfare state to new circumstances. In short, many of the reforms described in Chapter 4 are just the type of reforms that Langby (1984) suggested that Swedish politicians would not be able to agree on.[6]

Third, many threats and challenges were correctly identified and analysed, and remain still today. This holds, for example, for the way in which

---

[6] To be fair, it is likely that this is what Langby was hoping for. Those who predict doomsday are probably not mainly interested in being proven right.

high tax wedges on labour affect the service sector, and how lack of labour market flexibility creates problems related to the structural adjustment of the economy.

The next sections describe the two exaggerated threats and then discusses some challenges that remain: the effect of high tax wedges, work incentives for low-income earners and increasing labour market segregation.

EXAGGERATED THREATS (I): GLOBALIZATION

Economic openness and globalization have repeatedly been described as threats against the welfare state. The mechanism suggested is that increased mobility of capital and labour will lead to skilled labour and/or capital leaving the welfare state, thus eroding the tax base. Additionally, increased labour mobility may increase so-called welfare migration, where people migrate to take advantage of the generous welfare programmes of high-tax countries. Together, these forces may trigger a race to the bottom for tax revenue and welfare state generosity.[7]

As already noted, there are no obvious signs of a race to the bottom in aggregate statistics on government size. The same conclusion appears in more detailed studies, such as Starke et al. (2008) and Mendoza and Tesar (2005).

Potrafke (2010) concludes that domestic aspects such as unemployment and government ideology are more important determinants of labour market institutions and deregulation processes in OECD countries than globalization. Very similar conclusions are presented by Brady et al. (2005) who study the effect of economic globalization on the welfare state in affluent democracies between 1975 and 2001 and conclude that the globalization effects are far smaller than the effects of domestic political and economic factors. Similarly, Dreher (2006) showed that globalization had no effect on taxes and social policies, albeit with one exception: globalization correlates with lower capital taxation, just as expected when capital becomes more mobile.

It is worth noting that taxation of capital has never been an important source of revenue for the welfare state. In 2013, 60 per cent of all tax revenue in Sweden came from taxes on labour, 28 per cent from consumption (value added taxes, VAT) and an additional 2 per cent from tax on real estate (see also Table 4.1). Thus, while it is true that capital has been

---

[7] See, for example, Martin and Schumann (1997), Strange (1996) and Sinn (2003).

highly mobile globally for a long time, it is also true that tax revenue from internationally mobile capital is not crucial for financing the welfare state.[8]

In fact, in contrast to the race to the bottom hypothesis, both case studies and cross-country comparisons tend to find that countries with large public sectors are often highly integrated into the world economy (Rodrik, 1997; Steinmo, 2003, 2010; Lindert, 2004). For some time, this pattern was explained using the so-called compensation hypothesis, according to which open economies develop large welfare states and corporatist institutions as a response to the volatility caused by economic openness and international markets (Katzenstein, 1985; Cameron, 1978). Recently, however, this explanation has been questioned. Kim (2007) notes that the relationship between economic openness and volatility is 'not only theoretically ambiguous but empirically moot' (p. 210), and concludes that more open economies are not necessarily more volatile externally or internally. Along the same lines, Down (2007) presents empirical evidence that trade openness in developed countries is actually negatively related to both GDP volatility and price volatility.

The findings of Kim (2007) and Down (2007) suggest that countries with large welfare states actually benefit from economic openness. Similarly, Iversen (2005) notes that economic openness may be especially important for countries with generous welfare states:

> Labor-intensive, low-productivity jobs do not thrive in the context of high social protection and intensive labor-market regulation, and without international trade countries cannot specialize in high value-added services. Lack of international trade and competition, therefore, not the growth of these, is the cause of current employment problems in high-protection countries. (p. 74)

Iversen's view is confirmed and complemented by empirical evidence in Epifani and Gancia (2009) who show that high-tax countries benefit from globalization via a terms of trade mechanism: production costs in high-tax countries are passed on to consumers globally because exporters in high-tax countries have market power and can increase prices to levels well above marginal costs.

In all, recent research suggests that countries with large welfare states and high taxes benefit from globalization and economic openness. Openness is important both because consumers and producers in high-tax countries benefit from being able to import both products and materials from the rest of the world, and also because exporting to the world market allows welfare states to specialize in high value-added services. Increasing

---

[8] Data on tax revenue from Ekonomistyrningsverket.

economic globalization thus emerges as a partial explanation of Sweden's economic performance.

EXAGGERATED THREATS (II): AGEING

Population ageing as a threat to the welfare state has been discussed a lot.[9] It is indeed true that many aspects of population ageing give rise to substantial challenges for the welfare state, such as the financing of pensions, elder care and health care. As shown by Bengtsson and Scott (2010), however, the biggest challenge comes not from increased longevity but rather from the transition from high to low fertility. This transition poses a challenge for *all* countries, regardless of whether they rely mainly on the market, the family or the state for welfare service provision. The difference is the mechanisms used for the transition. Market-based systems use market prices and adjustments through supply and demand, whereas welfare state-based systems operate through political decisions.

The fact that the demographic challenge is caused by the transition from high to low fertility means that to some extent, the problems associated with demographic changes are of a transitional nature. To see this, it is useful to illustrate the demographic challenge using stylized population pyramids, as shown in Figure 8.2 (adapted from Bergh, 2010). A population pyramid graphically illustrates the distribution of various age groups in a population, with the youngest at the bottom and the oldest at the top, with the width of the pyramid indicating the size of the population in different age intervals. The pyramid looks like a regular pyramid when the population is growing, as depicted in Figure 8.2(a). When fertility falls, there will be a period with relatively more old people in the population,

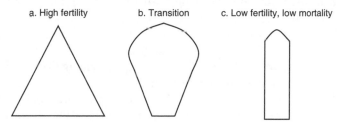

Figure 8.2   Population pyramids during the transition from high to low fertility

[9] For a recent survey with a focus in Sweden, see Bengtsson (2010).

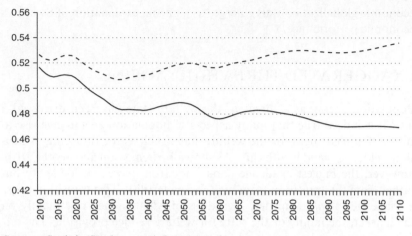

Source: Statistics Sweden, population prognosis.

*Figure 8.3   The share of total population in working age 25–64
             (continuous line) and including an increasing share of those
             aged 65–74 (dashed line)*

but those in working age will enjoy some alleviation from the fact that the
number of young to be supported is also decreasing. If the fertility rate
holds steady at just above two children per woman, the population will
stabilize.

Using the population forecast from Statistics Sweden, Figure 8.3 illustrates both the challenge and a likely solution. The continuous line shows
how the share of total population in working age (25 to 64 years old) is
expected to decrease over the period 2010 to 2110. While a population
forecast over 100 years of course is very uncertain, the accuracy is much
higher for the nearest future. The share of the population in working age
is falling, and will fall a lot during the 2020s.

The definition of working age, however, will change over time, and
already today we have seen an increase in employment for the age interval
65–74. Making the very brave assumption that this trend will continue to
grow with 0.5 percentage units per year, the working share of the population will evolve, as shown by the upper dashed line in Figure 8.3. This
illustrates the simple fact that as long as we are prepared to work a constant share of the total life cycle, the demographic imbalances that might
otherwise put the welfare state under pressure can be handled. Still, Figure
8.3 shows that the ratio will be less favourable during the 2020s and the
2030s, partly due to the big cohorts born in the 1940s.

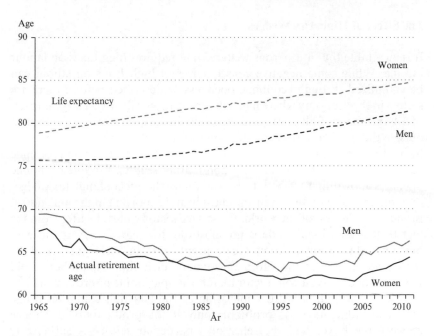

Source: OECD (retirement age) and Statistics Sweden (life expectancy).

Figure 8.4   Actual retirement age and life expectancy at age 50 (1965–2011)

Sweden's reformed pension system contains strong economic incentives to delay the retirement age, and Horngren (2001) argues that Sweden is well prepared to meet the demographic transition, by having taken actions at an early stage. As shown in Figure 8.4, the actual average retirement age that was falling for a long time has now started to increase.

REMAINING CHALLENGES

Having argued that the challenges from changing demography and increasing globalization have been somewhat exaggerated, it bears emphasizing that many inquiries into the problems facing high-tax societies did in fact identify a number of highly relevant factors. These factors remain relevant today, because reforms in these areas have been marginal. Simply put, the welfare state is not yet off the hook.

The Effect of High Tax Wedges

It is inevitable that a generous welfare state requires high taxes on labour income. While some negative consequences of high taxes on labour can be minimized through economic openness as described before, there are sectors in the economy where high labour taxation will have a large impact.

A large share of all work, and especially household work, is performed outside the market. Cross-country comparisons of industry-level employment also point to considerable scope for substitution of certain economic activities between the market and non-market sectors.[10] While economic openness allows high-tax countries to minimize the effect of high tax wedges on economic activity by importing cheaply and exporting high value-added products to the rest of the world, the service sector will still suffer from the fact that international trade is no substitute for many services. Instead, high rates of taxation of labour create incentives to shift a large share of the service production to the informal economy, including unpaid household work and a 'do-it-yourself' sector in, for example, home improvement.[11]

This is a straightforward application of the fact that a market transaction including taxes is profitable only if the productivity difference between the buyer and the seller of a particular service is sufficiently large.[12] Thus, for many activities when 'do-it-yourself' is a reasonable option, high tax wedges create incentives for illegal tax evasion (using black markets) or legal tax avoidance (using unpaid household work). Davis and Henrekson (2004) demonstrate that relative employment in the United States, with lower tax wedges and a more dispersed income distribution, was considerably greater in household-related services, such as repair of durable goods, hotel and restaurant services, retail sales, and laundry and household work.

No doubt, lifestyles that involve two income earners in married or cohabiting households increase the potential demand for many household-related services. If taxes hinder the development of a service-oriented economy, the unpaid household work becomes more important. Given the prevalence of traditional gender roles, women typically work fewer hours on the formal labour market and more hours in unpaid household work. Simply put, the high level of gender equality on the Swedish labour market is a result of comparing employment ratios between men and women,

---

[10] See Freeman and Schettkat (2005) and Olovsson (2009).

[11] This basic insight is important in the theory of optimal taxation. The theoretical results of Kleven et al. (2000) and Piggott and Whalley (2001) strongly suggest that the optimal tax structure involves a relatively low tax rate on those market-produced services that could alternatively be produced in the household sector.

[12] See Pålsson (1997) and Davis and Henrekson (2005).

rather than actual number of hours worked.[13] The fact that the seemingly high gender equality on the Swedish labour market is much less impressive once you look at the actual numbers of hours worked has been noted by Jonung and Persson (1993) in a paper titled 'Women and market work: The misleading tale of participation rates in international comparisons'.

From July 2007, a tax reduction lowers the price for households that purchase services related to cleaning, maintenance and laundry. As a result, the marketization of household services has increased, and proponents of the reform point to benefits both in terms of employment (especially for marginal groups on the labour market) as well as gender equality (because a market for household-related services is beneficial for two-earner households). On the other hand, some have argued that the tax reduction leads to a return of an unequal class society with maids, which Sweden left long ago (cf. Calleman and Gavanas, 2013).

In any case, the reduction can be seen as an attempt by policy makers to alleviate some of the consequences of high tax wedges on labour, using a targeted tax reduction for some very specifically defined services. Doing so should theoretically increase employment in the targeted area but it should also lead to demarcation problems, where providers use the system for purposes not originally intended. Finally, a targeted tax reduction typically spurs lobbying from interest groups who want to see similar tax reductions for other sectors. These consequences are hardly surprising, but Skatteverket (2011) argues that the tax reduction also affected the attitudes towards tax evasion, the idea being that when the legal prices decrease, it has become less accepted to hire people for these services without paying taxes.

Work Incentives for Low-Income Earners

During the 1970s and 1980s, the marginal income tax was a reoccurring theme in the political debate. This was hardly surprising, considering that the marginal tax for professionals could exceed 70 per cent up until the late 1980s (see Figure 4.2). After the 1991 tax reform, marginal taxes have been substantially lower for most income earners. However, for low-income earners on social assistance, work incentives are still very weak.

In Figure 8.5, marginal effects and the way in which disposable income varies with gross income among single people with no children in Sweden and the US are charted. Sweden and the US make for an interesting

---

[13] See Hakim (1996) who notes that in many European countries, the rise in female employment rates is due primarily to the creation of a new part-time workforce, while this has not happened in the USA. See also Henrekson and Stenkula (2009).

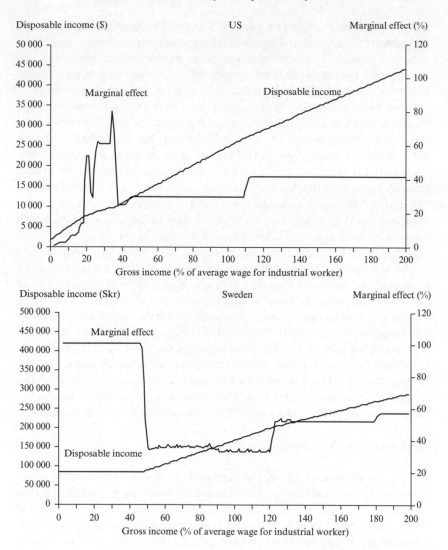

Note: The marginal effect measures how much of an increase in income disappears from the individual due to raised taxes and reduced benefits.

Source: OECD (2004).

Figure 8.5   The correlation between gross income and disposable income as well as marginal effects for a single person with no children in Sweden and the US

BOX 8.1   EMPLOYMENT AND UNEMPLOYMENT: SOME DEFINITIONS AND NORMATIVE INTERPRETATIONS

The employment rate is defined as persons in employment as a percentage of the population of working age, for example 15 to 64 years of age. The measure does not reveal how long people actually work, so the measure is sometimes complemented with a measure of the total number of hours worked over the year divided by the average number of people in employment.

High levels of employment in the sense that everybody who works should work several hours a day and many days a year does not, however, hold an intrinsic value. People typically value a combination of labour income (which requires work) and leisure time (which, by definition, is the absence of work). Each individual has his or her own view of what balance between work and leisure suits them best, and nothing says that material wealth is preferable to leisure or spiritual wealth.

However, what *is* certain is that what we consume must also be produced. The fact that a significant part of work earnings are taxed and used for public consumption does not change this. Material wealth includes welfare services such as health care, schooling and elderly care as well as computer games, clothes and fast food. Hence, it is not a problem if Sweden chooses to have shorter working days, longer holidays and a lower retirement age than many other countries – as long as we accept that the countries that work more can afford to have a higher level of material consumption.

Historically, technological progress has greatly increased productivity per hour worked, enabling people to enjoy both a higher standard of living as well as more leisure time. From an economic perspective, this is a consequence of leisure being a so-called *normal good*, that is, something we want more of as our income increases.

Employment problems in Sweden and elsewhere occur when people who wish to work (or wish to work more than they do) cannot find opportunities to do so. This is a problem both for the individual and for the surrounding society. The problem is captured by the unemployment measure, defined as all persons above a specified age who are without work, currently available for work, and who are seeking to work. Importantly, the unemployment rate is defined as all unemployed persons divided by the labour force (not the entire population). This means, for example, that Sweden, with close to 25 per cent youth unemployment, has almost 25 per cent of the labour force aged 15 to 24 looking for a job, which corresponds to roughly 12 per cent of the population in this age group (because students who do not seek jobs are not included in the labour force).[15] Finally, it is not completely straightforward even to interpret the unemployment rate normatively. Consider for example an unemployment rate of 5 per cent. If all the unemployed find a job within a month or two, then the economy is dynamic and a 5 per cent unemployment rate is no big problem. On the other hand, if all the unemployed have been unemployed for years, 5 per cent is much more problematic. The unemployment rate should therefore be complemented by long-term unemployment, defined as the percentage of total unemployed who have been unemployed for 12 months or more. In Sweden, roughly 20 per cent of unemployment is long-term unemployment, compared to 30 per cent for the USA and 44 per cent for the EU-15.

Summary:

- Employment rate: persons in employment divided by the population.
- Labour force participation rate: persons in the labour force divided by the population.
- Labour force: all persons who are either employed or unemployed.
- Unemployment rate: unemployed persons divided by the labour force.

comparison, since these two countries have chosen fundamentally different strategies to support those who cannot support themselves.[14]

[14] As put forward by Carone et al. (2004), Sweden is not the only country that has set up an unemployment benefit fund and a type of income support which create poverty traps – but the overall effect of the compensation levels and tax regulations nevertheless renders the Swedish marginal effects higher and affect higher incomes even when compared with other extensive welfare states in Europe.

The Swedish model combines high levels of taxation, also on low-level incomes, with relatively substantial income support which is reduced penny by penny against rising earnings. The disposable income for households with social assistance does not increase until social assistance has been completely withdrawn. The horizontal segment of the disposable income curve in Figure 8.5 for Sweden thus represents a poverty trap, where higher gross income does not lead to higher disposable income.[16]

Because the monetary work incentives are weak, support is typically conditioned on actively seeking employment and participating in various labour market projects. The intention is to increase the chances of getting a job, but because the individual has a strong advantage in terms of information he or she can, for instance, appear to be actively seeking employment by applying for jobs that he or she essentially does not want or cannot get.

The US strategy is very different. The support given to those who do not work at all is minimal, whereas people who work and have a low income are exempt from tax as well as being eligible for financial assistance. This system is therefore characterized by very strong incentives to work for those at the lowest income level and has been criticized for leading people to become 'working poor'.[17] The most significant difference between the Swedish and the US model, however, is that the poor in the US often have a job, albeit not a very well paid one, while poverty in Sweden by and large is caused by unemployment.

The Segregated Labour Market

In 2012, unemployment in Sweden was 8.2 per cent, which is very similar to the OECD average of 8.1. Sweden's employment rate was 74 per cent, well above the OECD average of 65 per cent.[18] These numbers are clearly not alarming. But the average rates hide substantial labour market segregation.

Figure 8.6 shows the relative difference between employment rates of the foreign-born and the native-born population in the OECD countries. In

---

[15] See further Statistics Sweden, 'Statistiken över ungdomsarbetslöshet är jämförbar', available at: http://www.scb.se/Pages/Article____353416.aspx, accessed 15 October 2013.
[16] In 2013, a minor change increased the work incentives for long-time welfare recipients by allowing 25 per cent of work income to be exempted in the social assistance calculations.
[17] See for example the illustrative account given by Ehrenreich (2001).
[18] The higher employment rate in Sweden is largely but not entirely due to female employment: for males the employment rates are: Sweden 76 per cent, OECD 73 per cent.

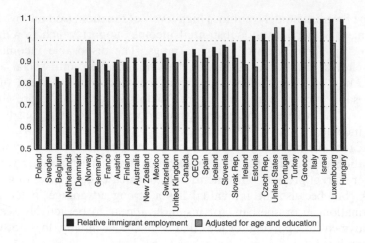

Figure 8.6   Immigrant employment relative to natives' employment

Sweden, the difference is larger than in most other countries. In 2009–10, 75 per cent of native-born Swedes aged 15 to 64 were employed, compared to 62 per cent of the foreign-born population. Thus, immigrant employment was 83 per cent of native employment, and as shown in Figure 8.6, only Poland had lower relative employment of immigrants. The OECD also report the difference in employment rates controlling for the age and education of the foreign-born population, and using that measure, Sweden is actually worse than all other OECD countries. The employment segregation can thus not be explained by immigrants in Sweden having a different age structure or education level.

Immigrants are not the only marginal group with problems on the Swedish labour market. Figure 8.7 shows a similar comparison among OECD countries for youth unemployment rates. In all countries, youth unemployment is higher than regular unemployment, but in Sweden and Italy, it is almost three times higher, and in Germany it is only 50 per cent higher.

Figure 8.8 shows Swedish unemployment in three different age groups since 1970: 16–24, 45–54 and the standard measure 16–64 years of age. It is clear that youth unemployment is more volatile, but also that the long-run trend is steeply increasing.

More than 30 years ago Björklund (1982) raised a warning flag regarding the continuously increasing unemployment in the group of 16–24-year-olds that began in 1965. With the devaluation in 1982 and the economic boom of the 1980s, the danger appeared to be over. Figure 8.8

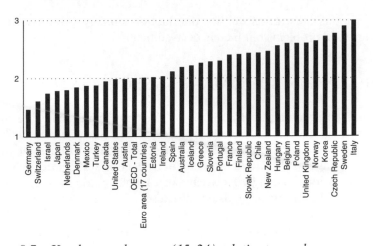

Figure 8.7   Youth unemployment (15–24) relative to regular unemployment (15–64)

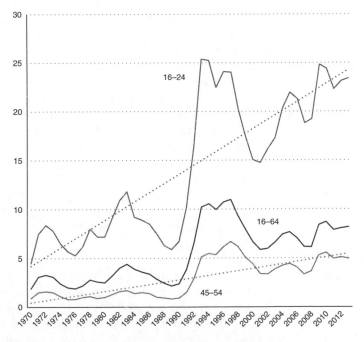

Note: For 2013, the value is based on the three first quarters.

Source: Statistics Sweden, AKU.

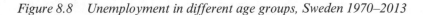

Figure 8.8   Unemployment in different age groups, Sweden 1970–2013

is yet another illustration that the devaluation strategy did not solve any fundamental problems but merely delayed them.

FIGHTING LABOUR MARKET SEGREGATION

Beyond the economic inefficiencies of unemployment, there are many adverse consequences for the unemployed person (see Jönsson, 2003 for an overview). Thus, it does not bode well that the level of unemployment among young people and immigrants in Sweden is systematically higher than the national average. How can such labour market segregation be mitigated? The answer depends on the causes of segregation.

Education vs. Deregulation

A harsh economic analysis of Sweden's segregated labour market suggests that for many who are looking for jobs it would not be profitable to employ them at current levels of wages, taxes and labour market regulations. The value of what they would produce is lower than what it would cost to hire them. Theoretically, the situation could be addressed by lowering wages and taxes, allowing more types of jobs, or by increasing productivity. There are downsides associated with all strategies. Lowering wage costs by lowering wages and/or labour taxes will only increase employment if people perceive these jobs to be preferable to the alternative, in many cases unemployment benefit or social assistance. The harsh economic solution would in those cases also include cuts to unemployment benefits and social assistance.

A similar reasoning holds for the option to allow more types of jobs. An EU survey concluded that Sweden has a lower share of jobs that do not require special skills than most other countries. This may be the result of regulations preventing these jobs from being offered – or it might be the case that these jobs are not offered because few people would apply for them.

The most obvious downside of a strategy based on deregulation and lower wage costs is arguably increasing income inequality. There are plenty of countries with lower starting salaries, lower tax wedges on labour and fewer labour market regulations, and they do typically succeed better than Sweden with regard to the type of labour market segregation described in Figures 8.6 and 8.7. They do, however, also have much higher income inequality.

The obvious alternative is then to increase productivity using education and training targeted towards those marginal groups who have trouble finding a job. This is in line with Sweden's strategy as described in the

Rehn–Meidner model (see Chapter 2). Another way of putting this is that the Swedish model requires people to be highly productive in order to fit into the labour market.

Increasing productivity though education and training is a well-tested strategy in Sweden, including both vocational training courses as well as the so-called Knowledge boost in the 1990s (*Kunskapslyftet*). However, the evaluations of these programmes that have been carried out point to only minor effects – see Stenberg (2005) and Calmfors et al. (2001). A likely explanation is that not even the most ambitious of education and training measures can replace the effect of actually being in a work place, learning from one's mistakes and making new contacts. Against this backdrop, it is hardly surprising that work experience is one of the most common requirements listed in job adverts. In many cases, the most important skills for finding a job are most easily acquired by having a job.[19] Finally, when the cause of low productivity is permanent injuries or health problems, education is less likely to work.

To sum up, the deregulation strategy means that labour market outcomes for marginal groups can be improved, but only at the price of increasing income inequality.[20] On the other hand, the education strategy has been a crucial part of the policies that have already been tried in Sweden and it seems unlikely that education and training is a panacea for labour market segregation.

Racist Attitudes and Xenophobia

While it is unlikely to explain youth unemployment, it is possible that racist attitudes and xenophobia can explain the segregated labour market for immigrants. Carlsson and Rooth (2007) provide relevant evidence of ethnic discrimination in the recruitment process by sending fictitious applications to real job openings. For ten job applications, Swedish-named applicants get called to interview three times, while applicants with Middle Eastern names only get called twice. Carlsson and Rooth (2006) confirm experimentally the existence of discrimination, but also estimate that ethnic discrimination is responsible for less than one-sixth of the native-immigrant unemployment gap.

Clearly, there is both racism and discrimination in Sweden. The same is true, however, for most other countries. To explain why labour market segregation of immigrants in Sweden is among the worst in the OECD,

---

[19] For example, many have pointed to Germany's successful apprenticeship system as an important explanation for the country's relative success with youth unemployment.

[20] For an empirical and theoretical analysis of the trade-off, see Adsera and Boix (2000).

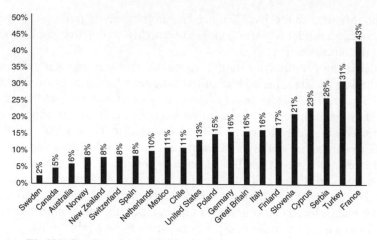

Source: World Values Survey, wave 2006.

Figure 8.9 *Share of the population who prefer not to have immigrants as neighbours*

xenophobic attitudes should be worse in Sweden than in other countries. Data from the World Values Survey suggest that the case is rather the opposite: the share of people in Sweden who stated that they would not like to have 'Immigrants/foreign workers' as neighbours, was only 2 per cent in 2006. As shown in Figure 8.9, all other countries covered by the World Values Survey have a higher share.

Similarly, Swedish anti-discrimination policies are ranked at the very top, together with Canada and the USA in the Migrant Integration Policy Index (MIPEX).[21] In all, it seems unlikely that discrimination and xenophobia is a major explanation of the segregated labour market.

Insiders and Outsiders on the Labour Market

Another theoretical explanation for young people's and immigrants' weak position on the labour market can be sought in the theory of insiders and outsiders, described by Lindbeck and Snower (1988). Insiders on the labour market are experienced, currently employed individuals whose positions are protected by rules and regulations, which makes it costly for companies to fire them and replace them with someone new. Outsiders lack this protection and are either unemployed or employed in the informal sector with no, or very limited, job security. Insiders have influence

[21] Available at www.mipex.eu.

over their work place by participating in wage bargaining (individually or through trade unions), through having influence over the work ethic and productivity of colleagues, through cooperation with management in generating production, sales and profits and by being able to threaten industrial action. Outsiders lack all of these channels: their strength comes from the potential to replace an insider with an outsider. But the more expensive it is to lay off, recruit and introduce new personnel, the worse the bargaining position for outsiders becomes.

The power that insiders have is further strengthened if the costs of unemployment are carried mainly by the state, as is the case in Sweden. In this case, insiders can use their bargaining power to get employers to increase wages for those with jobs, rather than to hire more people at lower wages. The costs for higher unemployment are covered by all tax-payers via unemployment benefit.

It is important to stress that employment security legislation on average does not have to lead to increased levels of unemployment. This is partly due to the fact that the extra costs which these regulations impose on employers can be shifted onto employees. The important outcome is the change in the structure of unemployment (see for instance Nickell, 1997 and Skedinger, 2010).

CONCLUSION: CAN THE CAPITALIST WELFARE STATE CONTINUE TO PROSPER?

Today, roughly 150 years after the free trade reforms in the 1860s, Sweden is doing relatively well economically. OECD (2012) notes that the Swedish economy has exhibited resilience in the face of international turbulence, thanks to sound macroeconomic policies and substantial structural reforms carried out since the early 1990s. The challenges mentioned by the OECD are similar to the ones discussed in this book: Sweden needs better labour market integration, and also needs to address the structural problems in the housing market. Among other things, the OECD recommends an increase in taxes on owner-occupied housing, a lowering of minimum wages relative to the average wage for groups at risk of becoming unemployed, and the introduction of a more efficient vocational and education system.

Roughly speaking, Sweden currently has the choice between the following strategies:

1. no further significant changes are made;
2. further reforms without decreasing the public sector;
3. further reforms which entail a reduction of the public sector.

The likelihood of Sweden choosing the first strategy should not be underestimated. As evidenced, much has already been done, and the immediate pressure for change in the form of a galloping budget deficit or some other crisis situation has now been averted. During the period 1996–2006, the political rate of reform was considerably slower than during the ten-year period beforehand, and after 2006 the major reform has been to lower taxes through the earned income tax credit. A plausible outcome of strategy 1 is that labour market segregation will remain or even worsen, with an apparent risk of unfortunate social consequences such as crime, social unrest and possibly also xenophobia.

The second strategy is the logical choice considering Sweden's history as a capitalist welfare state. In some areas, such as the labour market and the housing market, it is possible to increase competition and create likely efficiency gains without decreasing the size of the welfare state. But these markets may be the hardest to reform from a political perspective. When it comes to the taxation of low-income earners, the trade-off is more problematic, because lower taxation will mean a relatively smaller welfare state.

The third strategy seems unlikely. The universal welfare state enjoys stable or even increasing support among voters, and the demographic balance in 2020 and 2030 is likely to put pressure on public expenditure for healthcare and elderly care. Should it be chosen, Sweden will become less extreme and more like other countries when it comes to the size of the public sector. Which strategy Sweden will opt for is open to reader speculation – and for time to tell.

Appendices

APPENDIX A   THE REFORMS 1980–2000

1980 Consumers gain the right to use answering machines and fax machines from suppliers other than the state monopolist Swedish Telecom (Televerket).

A committee on credit policies is initiated. In an interim report from an ongoing commission on the currency regulation, several experts conclude that the restrictions on currency trade have not been effective.

1981 The Centre Party, the Liberal Party and the Social Democrats agree on a tax reform which puts an end to increasing marginal taxes.

1982 The committee on credit policies concludes that regulations are efficient in the short term, but do not produce the desired long-run effects.

1983 Liquidity ratios for banks were abolished.

1984 After six years of work, the committee on the pension system declares that the system is fraught with substantial problems and conclude that a reform is necessary.

1985 Interest rate regulations were completely abolished. The lending ceilings for banks and the placement requirements for insurance companies were abolished on 21 November, 1985 (sometimes referred to as the November revolution).

1988 New telecommunications policies: Swedish Telecom is stripped of its duties as an authority, and a new authority, the Swedish Board of Telecommunications, takes over the issuing of directives and managing of equipment.

A decision concerning transport policy prepares for competition on the railways: the National Rail Administration is set up to take over the infrastructure, and the railway network is divided into core rail networks and county railways in order to facilitate the competitive procurement of the latter.

1989 The currency regulations are abolished.

1990 The deregulation of domestic aviation is initiated.

Railway competition starts with BK Trains being granted permission to operate on certain routes in Småland region.

A far-reaching tax reform is implemented: tax bases are widened and tax rates are heavily reduced for both individual taxpayers as well as companies.

Sweden applies for membership in the European Community (EC).

The taxi industry is deregulated.

1991 Parliament gives the government the right to privatize a total of 35 state-owned enterprises or public utility companies.

The state enterprise the Water Power Board (Statens Vattenfallsverk) becomes the limited liability company Vattenfall AB.

The business CityMail is established. No legislation explicitly prohibits competition in the postal delivery sector.

Farming is deregulated and previously negotiated prices are gradually to be replaced by market prices. 14 billion SEK is set aside to facilitate the adjustment to market prices. Swedish EU membership, however, prevents full realization of the deregulation.

Headhunting businesses and recruitment companies are allowed to operate after obtaining special permission from the National Labour Market Board (AMS). Sweden withdraws from the ILO convention which prohibits recruitment activities for the purpose of profit making.

Government intervention in company investments, which commenced with the introduction of the investment funds in 1955, is brought to an end.

1992 The employee investment funds (*löntagarfonderna*) are phased out.

Commercial radio and TV is permitted.

Domestic aviation is deregulated, ending the monopoly of SAS and Linjeflyg.

New legislation gives local government more room to independently shape their organization.

School vouchers are introduced: local governments must pay independent schools at least 85 per cent of the municipal schools' average cost per student. The independent schools, however, are not allowed to charge any fees and they have to be recognized by the National Agency for Education.

First competitive procurement of county railways.

The State sells shares in Swedish Steel – SSAB (Svenskt Stål AB), the Nordic Satellite Corporation (Nordiska Satellitaktiebolaget), the plant breeding company Svalöf AB and the Swedish Waste Processing Corporation (Svensk Avfallskonvertering AB).

1993 AssiDomän AB is created from the former Swedish National Forest Enterprise (Domänverket) and National Forest Industries (Skogsindustrierna).

The level of compensation from the unemployment benefit fund is lowered from 90 per cent to 80 per cent.

New telecom legislation allows competition on the telecom market. Swedish Telecom (Televerket) becomes Telia AB.

Private employment agencies are permitted.

The Swedish Central Bank starts working towards the objective of limiting the annual increase of the consumer price index to 2 per cent.

The State reduces its ownership in the weapons industry company Celsius AB, from 100 per cent to 25 per cent state-owned. Further, the venture capital company Företagskapital AB is sold and several subsidiaries of the Swedish Geological Company (Sveriges Geologiska AB) are liquidated.

The main part of state-owned computer management and consultancy companies (SKD-företagen AB) are sold.

The government subsidies allocated to the municipalities go from being earmarked subsidies to being general subsidies, giving them greater freedom in deciding on public spending.

1994 Parliament decides on a new pension system.

The EEA treaty comes into effect, and consequently the EFTA countries are granted access to the EC internal market and free movement of goods, services, capital and persons.

The Swedish constitution is altered so that elections are held every fourth year instead of every third year.

The General Post Office (Postverket) becomes Posten AB.

The State sells off just under half of its holdings in AssiDomän AB. Procordia is divided up between the State and Volvo.

1995 A spending ceiling on the national budget is introduced. The spending ceiling is nominal and is set for three years at a time according to a rolling schedule. It also includes a budgeting margin allowing for fluctuations in the market.

Nordbanken, which was nationalized during the banking crisis, is refloated on the stock exchange through the State selling 34.5 per cent of the shares to the public.

Sweden becomes a member of the European Union (EU).

The State sells yet another part of Pharmacia.

1996 Introduction of a new energy policy, opening up the selling and production of electricity to competition.

1997 The new budget order with 27 expenditure areas is implemented for the first time. When the expenditure framework has been set, any increase in expenditure in any area (except the national debt interest) has to be financed within the framework.

Stadshypotek AB (the National Building Society) is sold.

1999 The so-called damage assessment for long-haul bus traffic is abolished. Previously, the coach companies were required to demonstrate that State Railways' (SJ) business would not be damaged by any given bus route. This regulation had gradually been relaxed during the 1990s.

The Securities Register Centre (VPC) is sold.

2000 The government sells close to one third of Telia's shares on the Stockholm Stock Exchange. The proposal to establish a National Audit Office is unanimously approved in Parliament, which thus provides Sweden with an independent national audit under Parliament.

APPENDIX B ANNUAL AVERAGE GROWTH OF REAL GDP PER CAPITA DURING THE NINETEENTH AND TWENTIETH CENTURIES IN SWEDEN

1800–1810	−0.4	1900–1910	1.9
1810–1820	0.1	1910–1920	0.8
1820–1830	0.8	1920–1930	3.4
1830–1840	0.6	1930–1940	1.6
1840–1850	0.9	1940–1950	2.5
1850–1860	1.2	1950–1960	3.2
1860–1870	1.2	1960–1970	4.5
1870–1880	0.7	1970–1980	1.9
1880–1890	1.0	1980–1990	1.8
1890–1900	1.4	1990–2000	1.5

Source: www.historia.se.

APPENDIX C   COUNTRIES RANKED ACCORDING TO DEGREE OF ECONOMIC FREEDOM

	1975		1985		1995		2000
1	Hong Kong	1	Hong Kong	1	Hong Kong	1	Hong Kong
2	Luxembourg	2	Luxembourg	2	Singapore	2	US
3	Switzerland	3	Switzerland	3	New Zealand	3	Singapore
4	Guatemala	4	Singapore	4	US	4	New Zealand
4	Panama	4	US	5	Ireland	4	Switzerland
4	US	6	Australia	6	UK	6	UK
7	Singapore	6	Canada	7	Switzerland	7	Canada
8	Belgium	8	Belgium	8	Australia	7	Ireland
9	Bahamas	8	Japan	8	Canada	9	Australia
9	Canada	8	Netherlands	9	Netherlands	9	Netherlands
9	Costa Rica	11	Germany	11	Luxembourg	11	Luxembourg
9	Germany	11	Malaysia	12	Finland	12	Denmark
13	Japan	11	UK	13	Chile	12	Finland
13	Netherlands	14	Bahrain	13	Denmark	12	Iceland
15	Malaysia	14	Oman	13	Germany	15	Germany
16	Australia	16	UAE	13	Norway	16	Australia
17	Iran	17	Taiwan	17	Iceland	16	Belgium
17	Venezuela	18	Panama	17	Malaysia	16	Chile
19	Cyprus	19	Finland	17	Mauritius	19	Oman
19	Mali	19	Mauritius	17	Panama	19	Spain
21	Australia	21	Austria	17	UAE	**19**	**Sweden**
21	South Africa	22	Bahamas	22	Taiwan	19	UAE
21	UK	22	Ireland	23	Belgium	23	Costa Rica
24	Barbados	22	Pap. New Guinea	23	Portugal	23	El Salvador
24	Denmark	25	Honduras	**23**	**Sweden**	23	Japan
24	Finland	**25**	**Sweden**	26	Philippines	23	Mauritius
24	Ireland	25	Venezuela	26	Thailand	23	Portugal
24	Thailand	28	Denmark	28	Australia	28	Argentina
29	Greece	28	Indonesia	28	El Salvador	28	Bahrain
29	Mexico	28	New Zealand	28	Japan	28	Botswana
29	Niger	28	Norway	28	Oman	28	Norway
29	Spain	28	Thailand	28	Paraguay	28	Panama
29	Taiwan	33	Barbados	28	Spain	28	Taiwan
34	France	33	Uruguay	34	Bahrain	34	Estonia
34	New Zealand	35	Chile	34	Costa Rica	34	Italy
36	Ecuador	35	Fiji	34	Guatemala	34	Philippines
36	Malaysia	35	France	37	Bolivia	37	France
38	Fiji	35	Paraguay	37	France	37	Jamaica
38	Mauritius	35	Spain	39	Argentina	37	Jordan

	1975		1985		1995		2000
38	Norway	40	Botswana	39	Trinidad & Tobago	37	Trinidad & Tobago
38	Sierra Leone	40	Cameroon	41	Honduras	41	Greece
38	South Korea	40	Jordan	41	Malta	41	Peru
43	Italy	40	South Korea	43	Italy	43	Guyana
43	Morocco	44	Belize	43	Jamaica	43	Malaysia
43	Philippines	44	Italy	45	Botswana	43	South Africa
43	**Sweden**	46	Bulgaria	45	Indonesia	46	Bolivia

APPENDIX D   SWEDEN'S TWENTIETH-CENTURY GOVERNMENTS

Period	Prime Minister	Type of government
12 Sept. 1900–5 July 1902	Fredrik von Otter	Right-wing
5 July 1902–14 Apr. 1905	Erik Gustaf Boström	Right-wing
13 Apr. 1905–2 Aug. 1905	Johan Ramstedt	Caretaker government
2 Aug. 1905–7 Nov. 1905	Christian Lundberg	Right-wing collective government
7 Nov. 1905–29 May 1906	Karl Staaff	Liberal
29 May 1906–7 Oct. 1911	Arvid Lindman	Conservative
7 Oct. 1911–17 Feb. 1914	Karl Staaff	Liberal
17 Feb. 1914–30 Mar. 1917	Hjalmar Hammarskjöld	Conservative
30 Mar. 1917–19 Oct. 1917	Carl Swartz	Conservative
19 Oct. 1917–10 Mar. 1920	Nils Edén	Coalition: Liberal, Social Democratic
10 Mar. 1920–27 Oct. 1920	Hjalmar Branting	Social Democratic
27 Oct. 1920–23 Feb. 1921	Louis De Geer (dy)	Caretaker government
23 Feb. 1921–13 Oct. 1921	Oscar von Sydow	Caretaker government
13 Oct. 1921–19 April 1923	Hjalmar Branting	Social Democratic
19 Apr. 1923–18 Oct. 1924	Ernst Trygger	Conservative
18 Oct. 1924–24 Jan.1925	Hjalmar Branting	Conservative
24 Jan. 1925–7 June 1926	Rickard Sandler	Social Democratic
7 June 1926–2 Oct.1928	Carl Gustaf Ekman	Coalition: Laissez-faire, Liberal
2 Oct. 1928–7 June 1930	Arvid Lindman	Conservative
7 June 1930–6 Aug. 1932	Carl Gustaf Ekman	Laissez-faire
6 Aug. 1932–24 Sept.1932	Felix Hamrin	Laissez-faire
24 Sept. 1932–19 June 1936	Per Albin Hansson	Social Democratic
19 June 1936–28 Sept. 1936	Axel Pehrsson	The Farmers Alliance
18 Sept. 1936–13 Dec.1939	Per Albin Hansson	Coalition: Social Democratic/ Farmers Alliance
13 Dec. 1939–31 July1945	Per Albin Hansson	Coalition: Social Democratic/ Farmers Alliance, Liberal Party, Conservatives
31 July 1945–6 Oct.1946	Per Albin Hansson	Social Democratic
11 Oct. 1946–1 Oct. 1951	Tage Erlander	Social Democratic
1 Oct. 1951–31 Oct.1957	Tage Erlander	Coalition: Social Democratic/ Farmers Alliance
31 Oct. 1957–14 Oct. 1969	Tage Erlander	Social Democratic
14 Oct. 1969–8 Oct. 1976	Olof Palme	Social Democratic
8 Oct. 1976–18 Oct. 1978	Thorbjörn Fälldin	Coalition: Centre Party, the Moderates, Liberal Party
18 Oct. 1978–12 Oct. 1979	Ola Ullsten	Liberal Party

Period	Prime Minister	Type of government
12 Oct. 1979–19 May 1981	Thorbjörn Fälldin	Coalition: Centre Party, the Moderates, Liberal Party
19 May 1981–8 Oct. 1982	Thorbjörn Fälldin	Coalition: Centre Party, Liberal Party
8 Oct. 1982–28 Feb. 1986	Olof Palme	Social Democratic
1 Mar. 1986–26 Feb. 1990	Ingvar Carlsson	Social Democratic
26 Feb. 1990–4 Oct. 1991	Ingvar Carlsson	Social Democratic
4 Oct. 1991–7 Oct. 1994	Carl Bildt	Coalition: the Moderates, Liberal Party, Centre Party, Christian Democratic Party
7 Oct. 1994–22 Mar.1996	Ingvar Carlsson	Social Democratic
22 Mar. 1996–6 Oct. 2006	Göran Persson	Social Democratic
6 Oct. 2006	Fredrik Reinfeldt	Right-wing coalition: the Moderates, Centre Party, Liberal Party, Christian Democrats

Source: http://www.regeringen.se/sb/d/4393.

APPENDIX E   AVERAGE TAX WEDGE FOR LOW-INCOME EARNERS IN 2000 AND 2012 AND PROGRESSIVITY OF THE TAX SYSTEM IN 2012

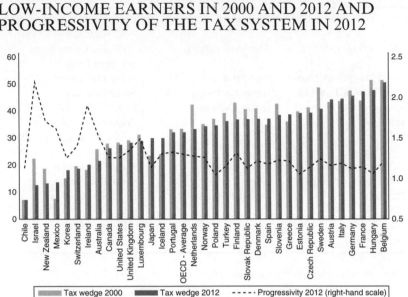

Note: Average tax wedge represents a single-earner household with no children earning 67 per cent of average earnings. Progressivity is calculated as the tax wedge for high-income earners (same household with 167 per cent of average earnings) over the tax wedge for low-income earners.

Bibliography

Abdiweli, Ali M. (2003), 'Institutional differences as sources of growth differences', *Atlantic Economic Journal*, 31: 348–62.

Åberg, R. (1989), 'Distributive mechanisms of the welfare state: A formal analysis and an empirical application', *European Sociological Review*, 5: 167–82.

Abrahamson, Peter (1999), 'The welfare modelling business', *Social Policy & Administration*, 33: 394–416.

Acemoglu, D., S. Johnson and J. Robinson (2001), 'The colonial origins of comparative development', *American Economic Review*, 91: 1369–401.

Adsera, Alicia and Carles Boix (2000), 'Must we choose? European unemployment, American inequality, and the impact of education and labor market institutions', *European Journal of Political Economy*, 16: 611–38.

af Kleen, B. (2009), *Jorden de Ärvde*, Stockholm: Weyler Förlag.

Agell, J., T. Lindh and H. Ohlsson (1997), 'Growth and the public sector: A critical review essay', *European Journal of Political Economy*, 13: 33–52.

Agell, Jonas, Henry Ohlsson and Peter Skogman Thoursie (2006), 'Growth effects of government expenditure and taxation in rich countries: A comment', *European Economic Review*, 50: 211–19.

Ahlin, Å. (2003), 'Does school competition matter? Effects of a large-scale school choice reform on student performance', Working Paper 2003:2, Department of Economics, Uppsala University.

Ahlin, Å. and E. Mörk (2005), 'Effects of decentralization on school resources', IFAU Working Paper 2005:5.

Ahlqvist, B. and L. Engqvist (1984), *Samtal med Feldt: Författarna Intervjuar Finansministern*, Stockholm: Tiden.

Andersen, T.M. (2008), 'The Scandinavian model: prospects and challenges', *International Tax and Public Finance*, 15: 45–66.

Anderson, R. and B. Soderberg (2012), 'Elimination of rent control in the Swedish rental housing market: Why and how?', *Journal of Housing Research*, 21: 159–82.

Andersson, Fredrik (2002), 'Konkurrens på kommunala villkor: En översikt', *Ájour*, 7: Svenska Kommunförbundet.

Andersson, Krister (2003), 'Utformningen av inflationsmålet och den penningpolitiska analysramen', in L. Jonung (ed.), *På Jakt efter ett Nytt Ankare: Från Fast Kronkurs till Inflationsmål*, Stockholm: SNS Förlag.

Andersson, Roland and Bo Söderberg (2002), 'Välfärdsvinster vid avveckling av hyresregleringen', *Ekonomisk Debatt*, 30: 621–31.

Andersson, Roland and Bo Söderberg (2005), 'Vad tänker Mona Sahlin göra åt den orättvisa hyresregleringen?', *Ekonomisk Debatt*, 33: 44–6.

Anton, Thomas J. (1969), 'Policy-making and political culture in Sweden', *Scandinavian Political Studies*, 4: 88–102.

Arthursson, M. and M. Ekelund (2004), 'Effekter av konkurrensutsättning av offentlig verksamhet', Report No. 2004-06-18, Svenskt Näringsliv.

Asoni, A. (2008), 'Protection of property rights and growth as political equilibria', *Journal of Economic Surveys*, 22: 953–87.

Barr, Nicholas (1998), *The Economics of the Welfare State*, Stanford, CA: Stanford University Press.

Barro, Robert J. (1990), 'Government spending in a simple model of endogenous growth', *Journal of Political Economy*, 98: S103–S125.

Baumol, William J. (1990), 'Entrepreneurship: Productive, unproductive, and destructive', *Journal of Political Economy*, 98: 893–922.

Belfrage, C. (2008), 'Towards "universal financialisation" in Sweden?', *Contemporary Politics*, 14: 277–96.

Bengtsson, T. (ed.) (2010), *Population Ageing: A Threat to the Welfare State? The Case of Sweden*, Berlin: Springer.

Bengtsson, T. and K. Scott (2010), 'The ageing population', in T. Bengtsson (ed.), *Population Ageing, a Threat to the Welfare State? The Case of Sweden*, Berlin: Springer, pp. 7–22.

Bentzel, R. (1952), *Inkomstfördelningen i Sverige*, Stockholm: IUI.

Bentzel, Ragnar, Assar Lindbeck and Ingemar Ståhl (1963), *Bostadsbristen: En Studie av Prisbildningen på Bostadsmarknaden*, Stockholm: Almqvist & Wiksell.

Berggren, N., A. Bergh and C. Bjørnskov (2012), 'The growth effects of institutional instability', *Journal of Institutional Economics*, 8: 187–224.

Bergh, A. (2004), 'The universal welfare state: Theory and the case of Sweden', *Political Studies*, 52: 745–66.

Bergh, A. (2005), 'On the counterfactual problem of welfare state research: How can we measure redistribution?', *European Sociological Review*, 21: 345–57.

Bergh, A. (2007), 'Skattefinansierad högre utbildning: Håller de fördelningspolitiska argumenten?', in N. Karlson (ed.), *Den Fria Akademin*, Stockholm: Ratio.

Bergh, A. (2008), 'Explaining the survival of the Swedish welfare state:

Maintaining political support through incremental change', *Financial Theory and Practice*, 32: 233–54.

Bergh, A. (2010), 'Towards a new Swedish model?', in T. Bengtsson (ed.), *Population Ageing: A Threat to the Welfare State?*, Heidelberg: Springer, pp. 109–18.

Bergh, A. and G.Ó. Erlingsson (2009), 'Liberalization without retrenchment: Understanding the consensus on Swedish welfare state reforms', *Scandinavian Political Studies*, 32: 71–94.

Bergh, A. and M. Henrekson (2011), 'Government size and growth: A survey and interpretation of the evidence', *Journal of Economic Surveys*, 25: 872–97.

Bergman, M.A., S. Lundberg and G. Spagnolo (2012), 'Public procurement and non-contractible quality: Evidence from elderly care', Umeå Economic Studies No. 846.

Bergsmark, Bengt (2006), 'Mest privat äldreomsorg i rödgröna kommuner', Kommunalarbetaren No. 2006-05-23.

Bergström, Fredrik and Mikael Sandström (2002), 'Wibes kritik är grundlös!', *Ekonomisk Debatt*, 30: 256–64.

Bergström, Fredrik and Mikael Sandström (2005), 'School vouchers in practice: Competition will not hurt you', *Journal of Public Economics*, 10: 351–80.

Berntsson, P. (2002), 'Den kvinnliga reservarbetskraften: Förlegad retorik eller aktuell politik? Exemplet den offentliga barnomsorgen', *Statsvetenskaplig Tidskrift*, 105: 238–49.

Beugelsdijk, Sjoerd (2006), 'A note on the theory and measurement of trust in explaining differences in economic growth', *Cambridge Journal of Economics*, 30: 371–87.

Björklund, A. (1982), 'Rehn/Meidners program och den faktiska politiken', Stockholm: Industriens Utredningsinstitut.

Björklund, A. (1993), 'A comparison between actual distributions of annual and lifetime income: Sweden around 1951–89', *Review of Income and Wealth*, 39: 377–86.

Björklund, A., M. Jäntti and M.J. Lindquist (2009), 'Family background and income during the rise of the welfare state: Brother correlations in income for Swedish men born 1932–1968', *Journal of Public Economics*, 93: 671–80.

Björklund, A., M. Lindahl and K. Sund (2003b), 'Family background and school performance during a turbulent era of school reforms', *Swedish Economic Policy Review*, 10(2): 111–36.

Björklund, A., D. Waldenström and J. Roine (2012), 'Intergenerational top income mobility in Sweden: Capitalist dynasties in the land of equal opportunity?', *Journal of Public Economics*, 96: 474–84.

Björklund, A., P-A. Edin, P. Fredriksson and A.B. Krueger (2003a), *Den Svenska Skolan: Effektiv och Jämlik?*, Stockholm: SNS Förlag.

Blomqvist, Paula (2004), 'The choice revolution: Privatization of Swedish welfare services in the 1990s', *Social Policy and Administration*, 38: 139–55.

Blomqvist, Paula and Bo Rothstein (2000), *Välfärdsstatens Nya Ansikte: Demokrati och Marknadsreformer inom den Offentliga Sektorn*, Stockholm: Agora.

Blomström, M. and A. Kokko (2003), 'From natural resources to high-tech production: The evolution of industrial competitiveness in Sweden and Finland', CEPR Discussion Papers 3804.

Boeri, T. (2011), 'Institutional reforms and dualism in European labor markets', in O. Ashenfelter and D. Card (eds), *Handbook of Labor Economics*, Vol. 4, Amsterdam: Elsevier, pp. 1173–236.

Böhlmark, A. and H. Holmlund (2011), *20 År med Förändringar i Skolan: Vad har hänt med Likvärdigheten?*, Stockholm: SNS Förlag.

Böhlmark, A. and M. Lindahl (2012), 'Independent schools and long-run educational outcomes: Evidence from Sweden's large scale voucher reform', CESIfo Working Paper 3866.

Böhlmark, A., E. Grönqvist and J. Vlachos (2012), 'The headmaster ritual: The importance of management for school outcomes', IFAU Working Paper 2012:16.

Bolin, Olof, Per-Martin Meyerson and Ingemar Ståhl (1984), *Makten över Maten*, Stockholm: SNS.

Borg, A. (1992), *Generell Välfärdspolitik: Bara Magiska ord?*, Stockholm: City University Press.

Boverket (2011), 'De Allmännyttiga Bostadsföretagens Utveckling och Roll på Bostadsmarknaden', Report No. 2011:21, Boverket.

Bradley, David, Evelyne Huber, Stephanie Moller, Francois Nielsen and John D. Stephens (2003), 'Distribution and redistribution in postindustrial democracies', *World Politics*, 55: 193–228.

Brady, D. and B. Sosnaud (2009), 'The politics of economic inequality', in K.T. Leicht and J.C. Jenkins (eds), *Handbook of Politics*, New York: Springer.

Brady, D., M. Seeleib-Kaiser and J. Beckfield (2005), 'Economic globalization and the welfare state in affluent democracies, 1975–2001', *American Sociological Review*, 70: 921–48.

Brännlund, R., A. Karimu and P. Söderholm (2012), 'Elmarknaden och elprisets utveckling före och efter avregleringen: Ekonometriska analyser', CERE Working Paper 2012:14.

Broberg, Oskar (2006), 'Konsten att skapa pengar: Aktiebolagslagens genombrott and finansiell modernisering kring sekelskiftet 1900', PhD thesis in Economic History, Gothenburg School of Economics.

Brunello, G., M. Fort and G. Weber (2009), 'Changes in compulsory schooling, education and the distribution of wages in Europe', *The Economic Journal*, 119: 516–39.

Calleman, C. and A. Gavanas (2013), *Rena Hem på Smutsiga Villkor? Hushållstjänster, Migration och Globalisering*, Gothenburg and Stockholm: Makadam Förlag.

Calltorp, J. (2008), *Ersättningssystem inom Hälso- och Sjukvården: En Kunskapsöversikt baserad på Internationella Erfarenheter*, Stockholm: Sveriges Kommuner och Landsting.

Calmfors, Lars, Anders Forslund and Maria Hemström (2001), 'Does active labour market policy work? Lessons from the Swedish experiences', *Swedish Economic Policy Review*, 8: 61–124.

Cameron, D.R. (1978), 'The expansion of the public economy: A comparative analysis', *American Political Science Review*, 72: 1243–61.

Canning, David and Peter Pedroni (2004), 'The effect of infrastructure on long run economic growth', mimeo, November.

Carlsson, M. and D-O. Rooth (2007), 'Evidence of ethnic discrimination in the Swedish labor market using experimental data', *Labour Economics*, 14: 716–29.

Carlsson, M. and D-O. Rooth (2006), 'Evidence of ethnic discrimination in the Swedish labor market using experimental data', Institute for the Study of Labor (IZA), Discussion Paper No. 2281.

Carone, G., H. Immervoll, D. Paturot and A. Salomäki (2004), 'Indicators of unemployment and low-wage traps: Marginal effective tax rates on employment incomes', OECD Social Employment and Migration Working Papers No. 18, Paris: OECD Publishing.

Castles, Francis G. (2004), *The Future of the Welfare State Crisis Myths and Crisis Realities*, Oxford Scholarship Online: Oxford University Press.

Chou, S-Y. (2002), 'Asymmetric information, ownership and quality of care: An empirical analysis of nursing homes', *Journal of Health Economics*, 21: 293–311.

Cox, R. (2004), 'The path-dependency of an idea: Why Scandinavian welfare states remain distinct', *Social Policy and Administration*, 38: 204–19.

D'Agostino, Antonello, Roberta Serafin and Melanie Ward-Warmedinger (2006), 'Sectoral explanations of employment in Europe: The role of services', Working Paper No. 625, European Central Bank.

Dansk Industri (2002), 'Migration and integration: The Danish experience in an international perspective', Copenhagen: Dansk Industri.

Davis, S.J. and M. Henrekson (2004), 'Tax effects on work activity, industry mix and shadow economy size: Evidence from rich-country comparisons', NBER Working Papers No. 10509.

Davis, S.J. and M. Henrekson (2005), 'Tax effects on work activity, industry mix and shadow economy size: Evidence from rich country comparisons', in R. Gómez-Salvador et al. (eds), *Labour Supply and Incentives to Work in Europe*, Cheltenham, UK and Northampton, MA, USA: Edward Elgar, pp. 44–111.

Dawson, J.W. (2003), 'Causality in the freedom–growth relationship', *European Journal of Political Economy*, 19: 479–95.

De Soto, Hernando (2000), *The Mystery of Capital: Why Capitalism Triumphs in the West and Fails Everywhere Else*, New York: Basic Books.

Demsetz, H. (1967), 'Toward a theory of property rights', *American Economic Review*, 57: 347–59.

Departementsserien (1988), 'Alternativ i jordbrukspolitiken', DS 1988:54, Stockholm: Expertgruppen för studier i offentlig ekonomi (ESO), Allmänna Förlaget.

Domberger, S. and P. Jensen (1997), 'Contracting out by the public sector: Theory, evidence, prospects', *Oxford Review of Economic Policy*, 13: 67–78.

Domberger, S. and S. Rimmer (1994), 'Competitive tendering and contracting in the public sector: A survey', *International Journal of the Economics of Business*, 1: 439–54.

Domberger, S., C. Hall and E.A.L. Li (1995), 'The determinants of price and quality in competitively tendered contracts', *Economic Journal*, 105: 1454–70.

Doucouliagos, C. and M.A. Ulubasoglu (2006), 'Economic freedom and economic growth: Does specification make a difference?', *European Journal of Political Economy*, 22: 60–81.

Down, I. (2007), 'Trade openness, country size and economic volatility: The compensation hypothesis revisited', *Business and Politics*, 9: 1–20.

Dreher, A. (2006), 'The influence of globalization on taxes and social policy: An empirical analysis for OECD countries', *European Journal of Political Economy*, 22: 179–201.

Ds 1988:54, 'Alternativ i jordbrukspolitiken', Stockholm: Fritzes.

Ds 1992:126, 'Statsskulden och budgetprocessen', Stockholm: Fritzes.

Ds 1996:37, 'Novemberrevolutionen: om rationalitet och makt i beslutet att avreglera kreditmarknaden 1985', Stockholm: Fritzes.

Ds 2002:32, 'Welfare in Sweden: The balance sheet for the 1990s', Stockholm: Socialdepartementet.

Du Rietz, Gunnar (2002), 'Skatterna och den ekonomiska tillväxten', Utredningsrapport 2002:6, Stockholm: Skattebetalarna,.

Easterly, W. and R. Levine (2003), 'Tropics, germs, and crops: How endowments influence economic development', *Journal of Monetary Economics*, 50: 3–39.

Edebalk, Per Gunnar (2000), 'Emergence of a welfare state-social insurance in Sweden in the 1910s', *Journal of Social Policy*, 29: 537–52.

Edebalk, Per Gunnar (2006), 'Sjukpenning och sjuklön: Samspelet mellan staten och arbetsmarknadens parter 1974–1999', Working Paper 2006:6, Socialhögskolan, Lund University.

Edgren, G., K-O. Faxen and C-E. Odhner (1973), *Wage Formation and the Economy*, London: George Allen & Unwin.

Ehrenreich, Barbara (2001), *Nickel and Dimed*, New York: Metropolitan Books.

Ekelund, Mats (2003), 'Sveriges glömda tillväxtnäring: Hälsa och sjukvård som möjlighet', Stockholm: Timbro Hälsa.

Elvander, Nils (1972), *Intresseorganisationerna i dagens Sverige*, Lund: Gleerup.

Englund, P. (1999), 'The Swedish banking crisis: Roots and consequences', *Oxford Review of Economic Policy*, 15: 80–97.

Epifani, P. and G. Gancia (2009), 'Openness, government size and the terms of trade', *Review of Economics Studies*, 76: 629–68.

Erixon, Lennart (2004), 'En balanserad hyllningsskrift trots allt?', *Ekonomisk Debatt*, 32: 41–4.

Erixon, Lennart (2006), 'The Swedish third way: An assessment of the performance and validity of the Rehn–Meidner model', work in progress.

Esping-Andersen, Gøsta (1990), *The Three Worlds of Welfare Capitalism*, Princeton, NJ: Princeton University Press

Esping-Andersen, Gøsta (1994), 'Jämlikhet, effektivitet och makt', in P. Thullberg and K. Östberg (eds), *Den Svenska Modellen*, Lund: Studentlitteratur.

Feldt, K-O. (1984), *Samtal med Feldt: Berndt Ahlqvist and Lars Engqvist Intervjuar Finansministern*, Stockholm: Tiden.

Feldt, K-O. (1991), *Alla dessa Dagar: I Regeringen 1982–1990*, Stockholm: Norstedts.

Feldt, K-O. (1994), *Rädda Välfärdsstaten*, Stockholm: Norstedts.

Figlio, D.N. and M.E. Lucas (2004), 'Do high grading standards affect student performance?', *Journal of Public Economics*, 88: 1815–34.

Finanskommitten (1863), 'Underdånigt betänkande angående Sveriges ekonomiska och finansiella utveckling, under åren 1834–1860, Stockholm.

Flygare, Irene A. and Maths Isacson (2003), *Jordbruket i välfärdssamhället 1945–2000*, Stockholm: Natur & Kultur.

Fölster, Stefan and Magnus Henrekson (2006), 'Growth effects of government expenditure and taxation in rich countries: A reply', *European Economic Review*, 50: 219–22.

Freeman, R.B. and R. Schettkat (2005), 'Marketization of household production and the EU–US gap in work', *Economic Policy*, 20: 6–50.

Galiani, S. and E. Schargrodsky (2010), 'Property rights for the poor: Effects of land titling', *The Journal of Public Economics*, 94: 700–29.

Garme, Cecilia (2001), *Newcomers to Power: How to Sit on Someone Else's Throne: Socialists Conquer France in 1981; Non-socialists Conquer Sweden in 1976*, Statsvetenskapliga Föreningen, Uppsala: Uppsala University Press.

Gerdtham, U.G., C. Rehnberg and M. Tambour (1999), 'The impact of internal markets on health care efficiency: Evidence from health care reforms in Sweden', *Applied Economics*, 31: 935–45.

Glaeser, E.L. (2003), 'Does rent control reduce segregation?', *Swedish Economic Policy Review*, 10: 179–202.

Glaeser, E.L. and E.F.P. Luttmer (2003), 'The misallocation of housing under rent control', *American Economic Review*, 93: 1027–46.

Goodin, Robert E. and Julian Le Grand (1987), *Not Only the Poor: The Middle Classes and the Welfare State*, London: Allen & Unwin.

Gottschalk, P. (1997), 'Income distribution in Sweden & the US', paper presented at the conference 'Labor Market Policy and Job Creation: Swedish and US Experiences', organized by the US Embassy, Stockholm, 20 May.

Grönqvist, E. and J. Vlachos (2008), 'One size fits all? The effects of teacher cognitive and non-cognitive abilities on student achievement', IFAU Working Paper 2008:25.

Grosskopf, G. and G. Rabe (1991), *Det Svenska Skattesystemet, Del 1, Individbeskattning*, vol. 3, Malmo: Beyronds Förlag.

Gunnarsson, Christer and Mauricio Rojas (2004), *Tillväxt, Stagnation, Kaos*, Kristianstad: SNS Förlag.

Gustafsson, J-E. and K. Yang-Hansen (2009), 'Resultatförändringar i Svensk grundskola', in *Vad Påverkar Resultaten i Svensk Grundskola? Kunskapsöversikt om Betydelsen av Olika Faktorer*, Stockholm: Skolverket.

Gwartney, J. and R. Lawson (2003), 'Economic freedom of the World Annual Report', Vancouver, BC: The Fraser Institute.

Hakim, C. (1996), *Key Issues in Women's Work*, London: Athlone Press.

Hamada, H., M. Sekimoto and Y. Imanaka (2012), 'Effects of the per diem prospective payment system with DRG-like grouping system (DPC/PDPS) on resource usage and healthcare quality in Japan', *Health Policy*, 107: 194–201.

Hansson, Åsa (2006), 'Svensk skattepolitik: Från Pomperipossa via århundradets skattereform till värnskattens utdragna avskaffande', Stockholm: Ratio.

Hansson, Pontus and Lars Jonung (2000), 'Det finansiella systemet och den ekonomiska tillväxten: Svenska erfarenheter 1834–1991', Appendix of SOU 2000:11, Finanssektorns Framtid.

Hanushek, E., J. Kain, J. Markman and S. Rivkin (2003), 'Does peer ability affect student achievement?', *Journal of Applied Econometrics*, 18: 527–44.

Hart, O., A. Shlefier and R. Vishny (1997), 'The proper scope of government: Theory and an application to prisons', *Quarterly Journal of Economics*, 112: 1127–61.

Heckelman, J.C. (2000), 'Economic freedom and economic growth: A short-run causal investigation', *Journal of Applied Economics*, 3: 71–91.

Heckscher, E.F. (1942), *Svenskt Arbete och Liv från Medeltiden till Nutiden*, Stockholm: Albert Bonniers Förlag.

Hedlund, S. and M. Lundahl (1985), *Beredskap eller Protektionism?*, Stockholm: Liber.

Henrekson, M. (1992), *Sveriges Tillväxtproblem*, Kristianstad: SNS Förlag.

Henrekson, M. (1996a), *Företagandets Villkor: Spelregler för Sysselsättning och Tillväxt*, Stockholm: SNS Förlag.

Henrekson, M. (1996b), 'Sweden's relative economic performance: Lagging behind or staying on top?', *The Economic Journal*, 106: 1747–59.

Henrekson, M. (1999), 'Sveriges ekonomiska tillväxt och samhällsforskarnas objektivitet', *Sociologisk Forskning*, 68–79.

Henrekson, M. (2000), 'När började Sverige släpa efter? Kommentar till Olle Krantz', *Ekonomisk Debatt*, 28: 355–7.

Henrekson, M. and U. Jakobsson (2001), 'Where Schumpeter was nearly right: The Swedish model and capitalism, socialism and democracy', *Journal of Evolutionary Economics*, 11: 331–58.

Henrekson, M. and D. Johansson (1997), 'På spaning efter de mellanstora företagen', *Ekonomisk Debatt*, 25: 217–27.

Henrekson, M. and J. Roine (2006), 'Promoting entrepreneurship in the welfare state', in D.B. Audretsch, I. Grilo and R. Thurik (eds), *The Handbook of Entrepreneurship Policy*, Cheltenham, UK and Northampton, MA, USA: Edward Elgar, forthcoming.

Henrekson, M. and M. Stenkula (2006), 'Företagsstruktur och nyföretagande i Sverige', Expertrapport till Kris- och framtidskommissionen, Svenskt Näringsliv.

Henrekson, M. and M. Stenkula (2009), 'Why are there so few female top executives in egalitarian welfare states?', *The Independent Review*, 14: 239–70.

Henricson, Ingvar and Hans Lindblad (1995), *Tur och Retur Amerika: Utvandrare som Förändrade Sverige*, Stockholm: Fischer & Co.

Horngren, L. (2001), 'Pension reform: The Swedish case', *Journal of Pensions Management*, 7: 131–8.

Hoxby, C. (2003), 'School choice and school competition: Evidence from the United States', *Swedish Economic Policy Review*, 10: 11–65.

Industry Commission (1996), 'Competitive tendering and contracting out by public sector agencies', Report No. 48, Melbourne: Australian Government Publishing Service.

Integrationsverket (2004), 'Statistikrapport 2004', Integrationsverket.

Iversen, T. (2005), *Capitalism, Democracy and Welfare*, Cambridge, MA: Cambridge University Press.

Jakobsson, Ulf (2004), 'Rehn–Meidner modellen in memoriam', *Ekonomisk Debatt*, 32: 36–40.

Johansson, Dan and Nils Karlson (2006), *Svensk Utvecklingskraft*, Stockholm: Ratio.

Johansson, M. (2006), 'Inkomst och ojämlikhet i Sverige 1951–2002', Arbetsrapport No. 2006:3, Institutet för Framtidsstudier.

Johnson, Anders (1997), *Inte bara Valloner: Invandrare i Svenskt Näringsliv under 1000 År*, Stockholm: Timbro.

Johnson, B. (2010), *Kampen om Sjukfrånvaron*, Halmstad: Arkiv Förlag.

Jönsson, Leif Roland (2003), 'Arbetslöshet, ekonomi och skam: Om att vara arbetslös i dagens Sverige', Lund Dissertations in Social Work 14.

Jonung, C. and I. Persson (1993), 'Women and market work: The misleading tale of participation rates in international comparisons', *Work Employment Society*, 7: 259–74.

Jörberg, L. (1976), 'The industrial revolution in the Nordic countries', in C.M. Cipolla (ed.), *The Emergence of Industrial Societies*, New York: Harvester Press, pp. 375–485.

Jordahl, H. (2008), 'Economic inequality', in G.T. Svendsen and G.L.H. Svendsen (eds), *Handbook of Social Capital*, Cheltenham, UK and Northampton, MA, USA: Edward Elgar.

Jordahl, H. (ed.) (2013), *Välfärdstjänster i Privat Regi: Framväxt och Drivkrafter*, Stockholm: SNS Förlag.

Jordahl, Henrik (2006), 'Avregleringar, entreprenadupphandlingar, kundvalsmodeller och vouchersystem', *The Swedish Model*, Report No. 9, Ratio.

Jörnmark, Jan (2002), 'Företag och företagande i Sverige', in L. Andersson-Skog and O. Krantz (eds), *Omvandlingens Sekel*, Stockholm: Studentlitteratur, pp. 145–72.

Jörnmark, Jan (2004), *Skogen, Staten och Kapitalisterna*, Lund: Studentlitteratur.

Josefsson, Dennis (2006), *Refomerna som förändrade Sverige*, Stockholm: Ratio.

Källström, Staffan (1991), 'En filosof i politiken: Vilhelm Lundstedt och äganderätten', Idéhistoriska Uppsatser, vol. 23, Stockholm University, Department for History of Ideas.

Kask, Peeter-Jaan (1997), *Vägen in i och ut ur Krisen: Ekonomisk Politik från Feldt till Persson*, Stockholm: Raben Prisma.

Katzenstein, P. (1985), *Small States in World Markets: Industrial Policy in Europe*, Ithaca, NY: Cornell University Press.

Kautto, Mikko (1999), *Nordic Social Policy*, London: Routledge.

Kim, S.Y. (2007), 'Openness, external risk, and volatility: Implications for the compensation hypothesis', *International Organization*, 61: 181–216.

Kingston, C. and G. Caballero (2009), 'Comparing theories of institutional change', *Journal of Institutional Economics*, 5: 151–80.

Kjellberg, A. (2011), 'Kollektivavtalenstäckningsgrad samt organisationsgraden hos arbetsgivarförbund och fackförbund', Studies in Social Policy, Industrial Relations, Working Life and Mobility, Research Reports 2010:1, updated 2 May, 2011.

Kleven, Henrik J., W.F. Richter and P.B. Sørensen (2000), 'Optimal taxation with household production', *Oxford Economic Papers*, 52(3): 584–94

Knack, S. and P. Keefer (1995), 'Institutions and economic performance: Cross-country tests using alternative institutional measures', *Economics and Politics*, 7: 207–27.

Kommunförbundet (1999), 'Konkurrens för fortsatt välfärd? Om förekomst, omfattning, effekter och erfarenheter av konkurrensutsättning och alternativa driftsformer', Stockholm: Svenska Kommunförbundet.

Kondo, N., R. van Dam, G. Sembajwe, S.V. Subramanian, I. Kawachi and Z. Yamagata (2012), 'Income inequality and health: The role of population size, inequality threshold, period effects, and lag effects', *Journal of Epidemiology and Community Health*, 66: 1–6.

Konkurrensverket (2012), 'Val av vårdcentral Förutsättningar för kvalitetskonkurrens i vårdvalssystemen', Report No. 2012:2.

Korpi, Walter (1996), 'Eurosclerosis and the sclerosis of objectivity: On the role of values among economic policy experts', *The Economic Journal*, 106: 1727–46.

Krantz, O. (2000), 'Svensk ekonomisk tillväxt under 1900-talet: En problematisk historia', *Ekonomisk Debatt*, 28: 7–16.

Kreps, David M. (1990), *A Course in Microeconomic Theory*, Harlow: Harvester Wheatsheaf.

Ladd, H. (2002), 'School vouchers: A critical review', *Journal of Economic Perspectives*, 16: 3–24.

Langby, Elisabeth (1984), *Vinter i Välfärdslandet*, Stockholm: Askelin & Hägglund.

Lantto, J. (2001), 'NPM-reformerna och demokratin', *Kommunal Ekonomi och Politik*, 5: 29–43.

Larsson, M. and H. Lindgren (1989), 'Risktagandets gränser: Utvecklingen av det Svenska bankväsendet 1850–1980', Uppsala papers in economic history, research report.

Leigh, A. (2006), 'Does equality lead to fraternity?', *Economics Letters*, 93: 121–5.

Levin, H. (1998), 'Educational vouchers: Effectiveness, choice, and costs', *Journal of Public Policy Analysis and Management*, 17: 373–92.

Lewin, Leif (1992), *Ideologi och Strategi*, Lund: Norstedts Juridik.

Lindbeck, A. (2001), 'Lessons from Sweden for post-Socialist countries', in J. Kornai, S. Haggard and R. Kaufman (eds), *Reforming the State: Fiscal and Welfare Reform in Post-Socialist Countries*, Cambridge: Cambridge University Press, pp. 145–80.

Lindbeck, A. (2012), *Ekonomi är att Välja*, Stockholm: Albert Bonniers Förlag.

Lindbeck, A. and D.J. Snower (1988), *The Insider–Outsider Theory of Employment and Unemployment*, Cambridge, MA: MIT Press.

Lindbeck, A., S. Nyberg and J.W. Weibull (1999), 'Social norms and economic incentives in the welfare state, *The Quarterly Journal of Economics*, CXIV: 1–35.

Lindbeck, Assar (1998), *Det Svenska Experimentet*, Kristianstad: SNS Förlag.

Lindberg, H. (2007), 'The role of economists in liberalizing Swedish agriculture', *Econ Journal Watch*, 4: 213–29.

Lindberg, H. (2008), 'Politikbyte och idéernas betydelse reformeringen av den Svenska jordbrukspolitiken', *Historisk Tidskrift*, 128(1): 29–54.

Lindbom, A. (2008), 'The Swedish Conservative Party and the welfare state: Institutional change and adapting preferences', *Government & Opposition*, 43: 539–60.

Lindbom, A. (2010), 'School choice in Sweden: Effects on student performance, school costs, and segregation', *Scandinavian Journal of Educational Research*, 54: 615–30.

Lindbom, A. (2013), 'Socialdemokraterna och privat drift i vård, skola och omsorg: Två idétraditioner', in H. Jordahl (ed.), *Välfärdstjänster i Privat Regi: Framväxt och Drivkrafter*, SNS Förlag, pp. 189–220.

Lindert, Peter H. (2004), *Growing Public*, Cambridge: Cambridge University Press.

Lindgren, K-O. (2006), 'Roads from unemployment: Institutional complementarities in product and labor markets', PhD thesis, Department of Political Science, Uppsala University.

Ljunge, M. (2012), 'The spirit of the welfare state? Adaptation in the demand for social insurance', *Journal of Human Capital*, 6: 187–223.

Lucas, Robert E. (1988), 'On the mechanics of economic development', *Journal of Monetary Economics*, 22: 3–42.

Lundh, Christer (2002), *Spelets Regler: Institutioner och lönebildning på den Svenska Arbetsmarknaden 1850–2000*, Stockholm: SNS Förlag.

Maddison, A. (1982), *Phases of Capitalist Development*, Oxford: Oxford University Press.

Magnusson, Lars (2002), *Sveriges Ekonomiska Historia*, Stockholm: Prisma.

Marier, Patrik (2005), 'Where did the bureaucrats go? Role and influence of the public bureaucracy in the Swedish and French pension reform debate', *Governance*, 18: 521–44.

Martin, H-P. and H. Schumann (1997), *The Global Trap: Globalization and the Assault on Prosperity and Democracy*, London and New York: Zed Books.

Mauro, P. (1995), 'Corruption and growth', *The Quarterly Journal of Economics*, 110: 681–712.

Meagher, G. and M. Szebehely (eds) (2013), 'Marketisation in Nordic eldercare: A research report on legislation, oversight, extent and consequences', Department of Social Work, Stockholm University.

Meghir, Costas and Mårten Palme (2005), 'Educational reform, ability, and family background', *American Economic Review*, 95: 414–25.

Mehlum, Halvor, Karl Moene and Ragnar Torvik (2006), 'Cursed by resources or institutions?', *World Economy*, 29: 1117–31.

Meidner, Rudolf, Gunnar Fond and Anna Hedborg (1975), *Löntagarfonder*, Stockholm: Tidens Förlag.

Mendoza, E.G. and L.L.Tesar (2005), 'Why hasn't tax competition triggered a race to the bottom? Some quantitative lessons from the EU', *Journal of Monetary Economics*, 52: 163–204.

Meyerson, Per-Martin, Ingemar Ståhl and Kurt Wickman (1990), *Makten över Bostaden*, Kristianstad: SNS Förlag.

Molander, P. (1999), *En Effektivare Välfärdspolitik*, Stockholm: SNS Förlag.

Moller, Stephanie, Evelyne Huber, John D. Stephens, David Bradley and Francois Nielsen (2003), 'Determinants of relative poverty in advanced capitalist democracies', *American Sociological Review*, 68: 22–51.

Montin, Stig and Jonny Wikström (2002), *Moderna Kommuner*, Stockholm: Liber AB.

Moore, A. and T. Balaker (2006), 'Do economists reach a conclusion on taxi deregulation?', *Econ Journal Watch*, 3:109–32.

Myhrman, Johan (1994), *Hur Sverige Blev Rikt*, Stockholm: SNS Förlag.

Myrdal, G. (1978), 'Dags för ett bättre skattesystem!', *Ekonomisk Debatt*, 6: 493–506.

Nickell, Stephen (1997), 'Unemployment and labor market rigidities: Europe versus North America', *Journal of Economic Perspectives*, 11: 55–75.

Nilsson, Lennart (2004), 'Service och demokrati', in L. Nilsson (ed.), *Svensk Samhällsorganisation i Förändring: Västsverige vid millennieskiftet*, Gothenburg University.

Norberg, Johan (1999), *Den Svenska Liberalismens Historia*, Stockholm: Timbro.

Nordfors, Miriam (2006), 'Vad är den Svenska modellen?', Stockholm: Ratio.

Nordin, Martin (2006), 'Arbetsmarknadspolitiska undanträngningseffekter', Stockholm: Ratio.

Nordström Skans, O. and O. Åslund (2010), 'Etnisk segregation i storstäderna: Bostadsområden, arbetsplatser, skolor och familjebildning 1985–2006', Report No. 2010:4, Institutet för arbetsmarknadspolitisk utvärdering (IFAU).

North, D.C. (1990), *Institutions, Institutional Change and Economic Performance*, Cambridge, UK: Cambridge University Press.

North, Douglass C. and Robert P. Thomas (1973), *The Rise of the Western World: A New Economic History*, Cambridge, UK: Cambridge University Press.

North, Douglass C. and Barry R. Weingast (1989), 'Constitutions and commitment: The evolution of institutional governing public choice in seventeenth-century England', *Journal of Economic History*, 49: 803–32.

Nutek (2005), *Årsbok 05*, Stockholm: Nutek.

OECD (2004), 'Benefits and wages', OECD Indicators, Paris: OECD.

OECD (2006), 'Taxing wages 2004/2005', Paris: OECD.

OECD (2012), 'Economic survey of Sweden 2012', Paris: OECD.

Ohlsson, Per T. (1994), *100 år av tillväxt: Johan August Gripenstedt och den liberala revolutionen*, Stockholm: Bromberg.

Olovsson, C. (2009), 'Why do Europeans work so little?', *International Economic Review*, 50(1): 39–61.

Olsson, M. and P. Svensson (2010), 'Agricultural growth and institutions, Sweden 1700–1860', *European Review of Economic History*, 14: 275–304.

Östh, J., E. Andersson and B. Malmberg (2013), 'School choice and increasing performance difference: A counterfactual approach', *Urban Studies*, 50: 407–25.

Pålsson, A-M. (1997), 'Taxation and the market for domestic services', in I. Persson and C. Jonung (eds), *Economics of the Family and Family Policies*, London: Routledge, pp. 153–70.

Pierson, P. (2001), *The New Politics of the Welfare State*, Oxford: Oxford University Press.

Piggott, J. and J. Whalley (2001), 'VAT base broadening, self supply, and the informal sector', *American Economic Review*, 91(4): 1084–94.

Potrafke, N. (2010), 'Labor market deregulation and globalization: Empirical evidence from OECD countries', *Review of World Economics*, 146: 545–72.

Pressman, S. (2007), 'The decline of the middle class: An international perspective', *Journal of Economic Issues*, 41: 181–200.

Rauhut, Daniel (2002), *Fattigvård, Socialbidrag och Synen på Fattigdom i Sverige 1918–1997*, Lund Studies in Economic History, vol. 18, Lund University.

Riksförsäkringsverket (2003), 'Regionala skillnader i sjukskrivning: hur ser de ut och vad beror de på?', RFV Analyserar 2003:12.

Rodrik, D. (1997), *Has Globalization Gone Too Far?*, Washington, DC: Institute for International Economics.

Roemer, J.E. (2002), 'Equality of opportunity: A progress report', *Social Choice and Welfare*, 19: 455–71.

Roine, J. and D. Waldenström (2006), 'The evolution of top incomes in an egalitarian society: Sweden, 1903–2004', SSE/EFI Working Paper Series in Economics and Finance No. 625.

Roine, J. and D. Waldenström (2008), 'The evolution of top incomes in an egalitarian society: Sweden, 1903–2004', *Journal of Public Economics*, 92: 366–87.

Romer, P.M. (1990), 'Endogenous technological change', *Journal of Political Economy*, 98: 71–102.

Rosen, Sherwin (1995), 'Offentlig sysselsättning och den svenska välfärdsstaten', in R.B. Freeman, B. Swedenborg and R. Topel (eds), *Välfärdsstat i Omvandling*, Kristianstad: SNS Förlag, pp. 63–80.

Rothstein, B. (1992), *Den Korporativa Staten*, Stockholm: Norstedts.

Rothstein, B. (1998), *Just Institutions Matter: The Moral and Political Logic of the Universal Welfare State*, Cambridge: Cambridge University Press.

Rothstein, B. (2011), 'Anti-corruption: The indirect "big-bang" approach', *Review of International Political Economy*, 18: 228–50.

Rothstein, B. and A. Lindbom (2004), 'The mysterious survival of the Scandinavian welfare states', paper presented at the annual meeting of the American Political Science Association, 2 September, Chicago.

Rothstein, J.M. (2006), 'Good principals or good peers? Parental valuation of school characteristics, tiebout equilibrium, and the incentive effects of competition among jurisdictions', *The American Economic Review*, 96: 1333.

Runciman, W.E. (1966), *Relative Deprivation and Social Justice: A Study of Attitudes to Social Inequality in Twentieth-Centrury England*, Berkeley: University of California Press.

Ryner, J.M. (2007), 'The Nordic model: Does it exist? Can it survive?', *New Political Economy*, 12: 61–70.

Rynér, Magnus J. (2002), *Capitalist Restructuring, Globalisation and the Third way: Lessons from the Swedish Model*, London: Routledge.

Sandelin, B. and B. Södersten (1978), *Betalt för att bo*, Stockholm: Rabén & Sjögren.

Santesson-Wilson, Peter (2006), 'Lättare sagt än gjort? En översikt av politiska svårigheter vid välfärdsstatsreformer', *The Swedish Model*, Report No. 9, Ratio.

SCB (2004), *Perspektiv på Välfärden 2004*, Stockholm: SCB.

Schön, Lennart (2000), *En Modern Svensk Ekonomisk Historia: Tillväxt och omvandling under två Sekel*, Stockholm: SNS Förlag.

Selen, J. and A.C. Stahlberg (2007), 'Why Sweden's pension reform was able to be successfully implemented', *European Journal of Political Economy*, 23: 1175–84.

Shleifer, A. (1998), 'State versus private ownership', *Journal of Economic Perspectives*, 12: 133–50.

Sinn, H-W. (2003), *The New Systems Competition: A Construction Principle for Europe*, Oxford: Blackwell Publishers.

Sjögren Lindquist, G. and E. Wadensjö (2005), 'Inte bara socialförsäkringar kompletterande ersättningar vid inkomstbortfall', Expertgruppen för Studier i Samhällsekonomi, Report No. 2005:2.

Sjögren Lindquist, G. and E. Wadensjö (2011), 'Avtalsbestämda ersättningar, andra kompletterande ersättningar och arbetsutbudet', Report to the Expert Group on Public Finance (ESO), No. 2011:4.

Skatteverket (2004), 'Skattestatistisk årsbok 2004', Stockholm: Skatteverket.

Skatteverket (2005), 'Tax Statistical Yearbook of Sweden 2005', Stockholm: Skatteverket,.

Skatteverket (2006), 'Skatter i Sverige: Skattestatistisk årsbok 2005', Västerås: Edita.

Skatteverket (2011), 'Om RUT och ROT och VITT och SVART', Report No. 2011:01, Stockholm: Skatteverket.

Skatteverket (2012), 'Skatter i Sverige: Skattestatistisk årsbok 2012', Stockholm: Skatteverket.

Skedinger, P. (2005), 'Hur höga är minimilönerna?', Rapport 2005:18, Institutet för Arbetsmarknadspolitisk Utvärdering (IFAU).

Skedinger, P. (2010), *Employment Protection Legislation: Evolution, Effects, Winners and Losers*, Cheltenham, UK and Northampton, MA, USA: Edward Elgar.

Skedinger, P. (2011), 'Employment consequences of employment protection legislation', *Nordic Economic Policy Review*, 1: 45–83.

Skolverket (2007), 'PISA 2006: 15-åringars förmåga att förstå, tolka och reflektera: naturvetenskap, matematik och läsförståelse', Report No. 306.

Skolverket (2010), 'Rustad att möta framtiden? PISA 2009 om 15-åringars läsförståelse och kunskaper i matematik och naturvetenskap', Report No. 352.

Skolverket (2012), 'TIMSS 211', Report No. 380.

Smeeding, Timothy M. and Susanna Sandström (2005), 'Poverty and income maintenance in old age: A cross-national view of low income older women', Luxembourg Income Study Working Paper Series Working Paper No. 398.

Snower, D.J. (1993), 'The future of the welfare state', *The Economic Journal*, 103: 700–717.

Socialstyrelsen (2003), 'Konkurrensutsättning och entreprenader inom äldreomsorgen: Utvecklingsläget 2003', Stockholm: Socialstyrelsen.

Södersten, Bo (1991), *Kapitalismen Byggde Landet*, Stockholm: SNS Förlag.

Solow, R.M. (1956), 'A contribution to the theory of economic growth', *Quarterly Journal of Economics*, 70: 65–94.

Solt, F. (2008), 'Standardizing the world income inequality database', *Social Science Quarterly*, 90: 231–42.

Soltow, L. (1989), 'The rich and the destitute in Sweden, 1805–1855: A test of Tocqueville's inequality hypotheses', *Economic History Review*, 42: 43–63.

SOU 1945:63, 'Slutbetänkande avgivet av Bostadssociala utredningen', Stockholm: Fritzes.

SOU 1982:52, 'En effektivare kreditpolitik', official government report, Stockholm: Fritzes.

SOU 1987:6, 'Folkstyrelsens framtid', official government report, Stockholm: Fritzes.

SOU 1987:44, 'Livsmedelspriser och livsmedelskvalitet', official government report, Stockholm: Fritzes.

SOU 1989:33, 'Reformerad inkomstbeskattning', official government report, Stockholm: Fritzes.

SOU 1989:34, 'Reformerad foretagsbeskattning' official government report, Stockholm: Fritzes.

150   *Sweden and the revival of the capitalist welfare state*

SOU 1989:35, 'Reformerad mervärdesskatt m.m.', official government report, Stockholm: Fritzes.
SOU 1990:76, 'Allmän pension', official government report, Stockholm: Fritzes.
SOU 1991:13, 'Spelreglerna på arbetsmarknaden', official government report, Stockholm: Fritzes.
SOU 1992:38, 'Fristående skolor: Bidrag och elevavgifter', official government report, Stockholm: Fritzes.
SOU 1993:16, 'Nya villkor för ekonomi och politik', official government report, Stockholm: Fritzes.
SOU 1994:20 'Reformerat pensionssystem', official government report, Stockholm: Fritzes.
SOU 1995:104, 'Skattereformen 1990–1991: En utvärdering', official government report, Stockholm: Fritzes.
SOU 1997:131 'Lag om premiepension', official government report, Stockholm: Fritzes.
SOU 1999:136, 'Personval 1998: En utvärdering av personvalsreformen', official government report, Stockholm: Fritzes.
SOU 2000:38, 'Välfärd, vård och omsorg', official government report, Stockholm: Fritzes.
SOU 2006:86, 'Mera försäkring och mera arbete', official government report, Stockholm: Fritzes.
Ståhl, I. and K. Wickman (1993), *Suedosclerosis, Stockholm*: Timbro.
Ståhlberg, Ann-Charlotte (2003), 'Occupational welfare', in T.M. Andersen and P. Molander (eds), *Alternatives for Welfare Policy: Coping with Internationalisation and Demographic Change*, Cambridge: Cambridge University Press, pp. 189–206.
Starke, P., H. Obinger and F. Castles (2008), 'Convergence towards where: In what ways, if any, are welfare states becoming more similar?', *Journal of European Public Policy*, 15: 975–1000.
Statskontoret (2004), 'Avregleringen av sex marknader: Mål, medel och resultat', Report No. 2004:28, Stockholm.
Stein, P. (1991), 'Sweden: From capitalist success to welfare-state sclerosis', Cato Policy Analysis No. 160, Cato Institute.
Steinmo, S. (2003), 'Bucking the trend? The welfare state and the global economy: The Swedish case up close', *New Political Economy*, 8: 31–49.
Steinmo, S. (2010), *The Evolution of Modern States: Sweden, Japan, and the United States*, New York: Cambridge University Press.
Stenberg, Anders (2005), 'Comprehensive education for the unemployed: Evaluating the effects on unemployment of the adult education initiative in Sweden', *Labour*, 19: 123–46.
Stenkula, M., D. Johansson and G. Du Rietz (2013), 'Marginal taxation

on labor income in Sweden from 1862 to 2010', *Scandinavian Economic History Review*, forthcoming.

Strange, S. (1996), *The Retreat of the State: The Diffusion of Power in the World Economy*, Cambridge: Cambridge University Press.

Subramanian, S.V. and I. Kawachi (2004), 'Income inequality and health: What have we learned so far?', *Epidemiologic Reviews*, 26: 78–91.

Suzuki, K. (2001), 'Marketization of elderly care in Sweden', EIJS Working Paper 137, Stockholm School of Economics, Stockholm.

Svallfors, S. (2011), 'A bedrock of support? Trends in welfare state attitudes in Sweden, 1981–2010', *Social Policy & Administration*, 45: 806–825.

Svenska kommunalarbetareförbundet (2002), 'Solidaritet och valfrihet i välfärden', Report passed at the Association meeting in 2002.

Svenska kommunförbundet (2001), 'Valfrihet och kundvalssystem i kommunal verksamhet: Underlag för lokala bedömningar', Stockholm: Svenska Kommunförbundet.

Svenskt Näringsliv (2002), *Hur Nöjda Är Sjuksköterskorna*, Stockholm: Svenskt Näringsliv and VIAM.

Svensson, J. and R. Reinikka (2005), 'Fighting corruption to improve schooling: Evidence from a newspaper campaign in Uganda', *Journal of the European Economic Association*, 3: 259–67.

Swedish Ministry of Health and Social Affairs (2002), Ds 2002:32, 'Welfare in Sweden: The balance sheet for the 1990s', Stockholm: Socialdepartementet.

Therborn, Göran (1994), 'Nation och klass, tur och skicklighet', in P. Thullberg and K. Östberg (eds), *Den Svenska Modellen*, Lund: Studentlitteratur.

Thoursie, P.S. (2004), 'Reporting sick: Are sporting events contagious?', *Journal of Applied Econometrics*, 19: 809–23.

Thullberg, Per and Kjell Östberg (1994), *Den Svenska Modellen*, Lund: Studentlitteratur.

Timonen, Virpi (2001), 'Earning welfare citizenship: Welfare state reform in Finland and Sweden', in P. Taylor-Gooby (ed.), *Welfare States Under Pressure*, London: Sage Publications, pp. 29–51.

Titmuss, Richard A. (1974), *Social Policy*, London: Allen and Unwin.

Toft, Christian (2003), 'Evidence-based social science and the Rehnist interpretation of the development of active labor market policy in Sweden during the Golden Age: A critical examination', *Politics & Society*, 31: 567–608.

Trydegård, G-B. (2004), 'Welfare services for the elderly in Sweden at the beginning of the 21st century: Still in line with the Nordic welfare state model?, paper presented at 'Social policy as if people matter:

A cross-national dialogue' conference, 11–12 November, Adelphi University, Garden City, NY.

Tullock, G. (1967), 'The welfare costs of tariffs, monopolies, and theft', *Western Economic Journal*, 5: 224–32.

Uddhammar, Emil (1993), *Partierna och den Stora Staten*, Stockholm: City University Press.

Uslaner, Eric M. and Mitchell Brown (2005), 'Inequality, trust and civic engagement', *American Politics Research*, 33: 868–95.

Uusitalo, H. (1985), 'Redistribution and equality in the welfare state: An effort to interpret the major findings of research on the redistributive effects of the welfare state', *European Sociological Review*, 1: 163–76.

Vlachos, J. (2010), 'Betygets värde: En analys av hur konkurrens påverkar betygssättningen vid Svenska skolor', Report No. 2010:6, Konkurrensverket, Stockholm.

Vlachos, J. (2012), 'Är konkurrens och vinst en bra modell för skolan', *Ekonomisk Debatt*, 4: 16–30.

von Otter, Carsten (2003), *Ute och inne i Svenskt Arbetsliv*, Stockholm: Arbetslivsinstitutet.

Wengström, Erik (2006), 'Det svenska företagsklimatet: Himmel eller helvete?', Stockholm: Ratio.

Werin, Lars, Peter Englund, Lars Jonung and Clas Wihlborg (1993), *Från räntereglering till inflationsnorm: Det finansiella systemet och riksbankens politik 1945–1990*, Kristianstad: SNS.

Westholm, C-J. (2009), 'To our foreign readers', *Svensk Tidskrift*, available online: http://www.svensktidskrift.se/?p=2524, accessed 11 January 2013.

Wolff, Michael (1992), *Where we Stand: Can America Make it in the Global Race for Wealth, Health and Happiness?*, New York: Bantam Books.

Yitzhaki, S. (1982), 'Relative deprivation and economic welfare', *European Economic Review*, 17: 99–113.

Zak, Paul J. and Stephen Knack (2001), 'Trust and growth', *The Economic Journal*, 111: 295–321.

Index